9-97

W9-BRV-548

8.4

5.0

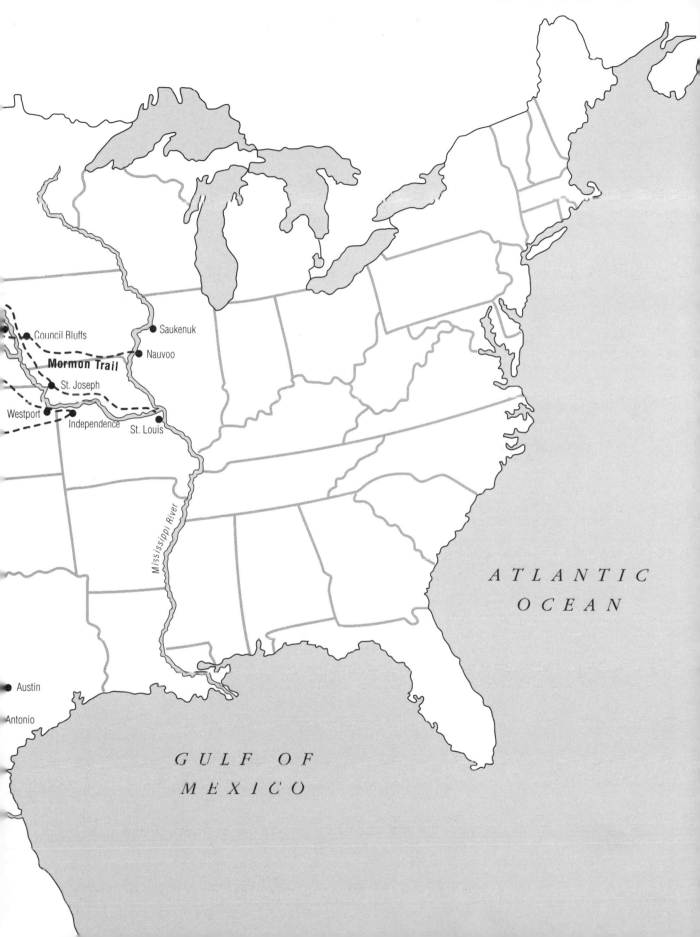

Council Bluffs

Saukenuk

Nauvoo

Mormon Trail

St. Joseph

Westport

Independence

St. Louis

Mississippi River

Austin

Antonio

ATLANTIC
OCEAN

GULF OF
MEXICO

Beyond the
Mississippi

Artist John Gast painted "American Progress" to symbolize—and romanticize—the country's expansion across the continent. While Indians and buffalo flee, a woman floats westward, stringing telegraph wires and leading farmers, miners, stagecoaches, and railroads.

Beyond the Mississippi

EARLY WESTWARD EXPANSION OF THE UNITED STATES

ANGELA M. HERB

LODESTAR BOOKS
Dutton   New York

Library of Congress Cataloging-in-Publication Data

Herb, Angela M.
    Beyond the Mississippi: early westward expansion of the United States / Angela M. Herb.
        p.   cm.—(Young readers' history of the West)
    Includes bibliographical references and index.
    Summary: Examines the exploration and migration of trappers, missionaries, and explorers west of the Mississippi after the Louisiana Purchase and the expedition of Lewis and Clark.
    ISBN 0-525-67503-5 (alk. paper)
    1. West (U.S.)—History—To 1848—Juvenile literature.   2. West (U.S.)—Discovery and exploration—Juvenile literature.   3. United States—Territorial expansion—Juvenile literature.   [1. West (U.S.)—History—To 1848.   2. West (U.S.)—Discovery and exploration. 3. United States—Territorial expansion.]   I. Title.   II. Series.
    F592.H46   1996
    978—dc20   96-47
                                                              CIP
                                                              AC

Published in the United States by Lodestar Books,
an affiliate of Dutton Children's Books,
a division of Penguin Books USA Inc.
375 Hudson Street
New York, New York 10014

Published simultaneously in Canada
by McClelland & Stewart, Toronto

Series development/book production: Laing Communications Inc.,
        Redmond, Washington.
Editorial management: Christine Laing
Editorial assistance: Heather Burns, Laura Dickinson, Emily Smith
Design: Sandra Harner

Printed in Mexico   First Edition   10 9 8 7 6 5 4 3 2 1

Contents

to Norm, Chris, and Sandi
for welcome opportunities, steadfast support, and good humor

and to Pete,
for steadying the keel at just the right times

Acknowledgments

Many thanks to the following individuals:

Mark Gardner, of Cascade, Colorado; John Findlay, associate professor of history at the University of Washington; Sean Jones, Emily Peterson, Leslie Rossman, Colin Trovato, and the many other 1994–1995 fifth-grade reviewers at Hollywood Hill Elementary School, Woodinville, Washington; Park Ranger Rick Edwards, Fort Vancouver National Historic Site; Susan Seyl, photo librarian, and the rest of the staff at the Oregon Historical Society, Portland; Laura Mills, archivist at the Jefferson National Expansion Memorial, St. Louis; Tim Noakes and Linda J. Long, of the Department of Special Collections, Stanford University Libraries; Bill Slaughter, archivist, The Church of Jesus Christ of Latter-day Saints, Salt Lake City; and Dave Merchant.

Introduction

The Lure of the Land

In the summer of 1540, Francisco Vázquez de Coronado rode up to a Zuni Indian village bedecked in a plumed helmet and a suit of gilded armor. The Zunis greeted the Spaniard with extreme reluctance, but no surprise; their scouts had been spying on the stranger's progress.

Over the past six months, the thirty-year-old nobleman had traveled north from Mexico over age-old Indian trails, leading more than three hundred Spaniards and one thousand Indians on horseback. His troop of conquistadors, or conquerors, were searching for Cíbola, a city rumored to be larger and more magnificent than Mexico City, with temples covered in gems. Instead Coronado found the stone and adobe village of the Zunis, whose culture was rich with corn, textiles, and pottery, but not the gold, silver, and jewels the Spanish sought. Nevertheless the conquistadors fought their way into the pueblo and claimed the region for their king.

The following spring, Coronado continued on, looking for another imaginary kingdom called Quivira, which he believed existed on the Great Plains. The conquistadors met the Apaches and other nomadic Indians of the plains as well as the Wichitas of the Arkansas River Valley, with their villages of grass lodges and fields of corn, beans, and squash. Still no cities of gold. Coronado led his men as far into the continent's interior as present-day Kansas, plundering numerous Indian villages but never finding the rich kingdoms he had dreamed of claiming for Spain.

After suffering a serious riding injury, the disillusioned leader returned to Mexico City.

Although they lost interest in the Great Plains, for the next two hundred and fifty years the Spanish continued to conquer lands along the Pacific Coast and southern rim of North America. They enslaved thousands of Indians and built missions and presidios in California, New Mexico, and Texas. The Spanish never questioned their right to claim the land and overtake native peoples. Like many Europeans, they firmly believed they were superior to non-Christians—that their god had given them dominion over all other creatures.

In time, the Spanish faced competition for control of the American West from the French, British, and Russians, as well as a fledgling nation: the United States of America. In the early 1780s, international traders discovered the value of the Pacific sea otter, whose furs brought fantastically high prices in China. The discovery led to a frenzied competition of trading ships from California to Alaska as well as a growing interest in the unexplored resources inland. By the turn of the century, the Spanish had largely withdrawn from the competition north of California to focus on their Mexican landholdings. In addition, the once-invincible nation ceded a large portion of its northernmost land claims—an 828,000-square-mile expanse known as Louisiana Territory—to France.

While Spain's presence in the area waned, the United States stood poised to expand. Since declaring its independence from Great Britain in 1776, the nation's population had swelled. Each year, pioneers looking for new land to settle pushed the U.S. frontier west toward the Mississippi River, which formed the border of Louisiana Territory.

Like the Spanish conquistadors before them, when Americans looked beyond the Mississippi, they saw an open and beckoning land. Despite the presence of hundreds of Indian nations with rich and distinct cultures, who had populated the land for thousands of years—from the deserts of the Southwest and the grassy prairies of the Great Plains to the high valleys of the Rocky Mountains and the salty beaches of the Pacific Coast—Americans considered the West to be an empty wilderness. And in less than fifty years, from the 1803 purchase of Louisiana Territory to the California gold rush of 1849, the nation would expand and conquer the West.

In 1845, a New York newspaperman named John Louis O'Sullivan coined the term Manifest Destiny to describe America's belief that it had a God-given right to settle and develop the West. "The American claim," the journalist justified, "is by right of our manifest destiny to overspread and to possess the whole of the continent which Providence [or, God] has given us. . . ." It was with this unwavering confidence that America headed west. ✪

The Nation Stretches West

Chinook Indians paddle out to greet Captain Robert Gray, May 1792.

1790–1799

October 1790
After more than two centuries of exploration and colonization efforts along the Pacific Coast, Spain begins to relinquish its claims to the Oregon country. King Carlos accepts a treaty with Spain's strongest rival—Great Britain—agreeing to share the Northwest and its valuable sea otter fur trade.

May 1792
American sea trader Robert Gray discovers the mouth of the Columbia River, giving the United States a claim to the Oregon country. Captain Gray also crosses paths with British explorer George Vancouver, whose careful mapping of the coast from California to Alaska gives the British greater control over the Northwest.

1793
Alexander Mackenzie, an explorer for the North West Company of Montreal, treks across Canada to the Pacific Ocean—the first white man to cross the breadth of North America by land.

1800–1809

April 1803
President Thomas Jefferson purchases Louisiana Territory from France, doubling the size of the United States.

May 1804
The Lewis and Clark expedition departs from Camp Wood, following the Missouri River in search of a route to the Pacific Ocean.

September 1806
Lewis and Clark's Corps of Discovery returns to St. Louis with much fanfare. In 28 months, they had covered 8,000 miles, bringing home detailed maps and information on 40 Indian tribes, 122 new animals, and 178 new plants.

> Capt. William Clark December 3d 1805. By Land. U. States in 1804–1805.

Carved on a pine tree by William Clark, shortly after arriving at the Pacific Coast

Lieutenant Zebulon Montgomery Pike

August 1805
Lieutenant Zebulon Montgomery Pike sets out to explore the headwaters of the Mississippi River, traveling first by boat then by dogsled on the frozen river. On July 15, 1806, less than three months after returning, Pike heads west again to explore the Red River. After crossing the border of Louisiana Territory—most likely to spy on New Mexico—he is arrested by the Spanish. In June 1807, Pike returns to the United States and receives some fame as an explorer. He is killed shortly afterward in the War of 1812.

1810–1815

Fall 1810
New Yorker John Jacob Astor sends two expeditions—one by land and one by sea—to the mouth of the Columbia River to compete with the British for the Pacific Northwest fur trade. When Canadian explorer David Thompson arrives at the river's mouth in 1811, he finds the Astorians have already built a crude trading fort. However, during the War of 1812, the Americans are forced to sell the post to his company.

June 1812
The United States and Great Britain declare war, arguing over the expansion of the American frontier as well as commercial trading rights on the Atlantic Ocean. In February 1815, a truce to the War of 1812 is reached with the Treaty of Ghent.

*Texas colonizer
Stephen Austin*

*A Rocky Mountain
trapper*

1820–1829

October 1818
In the Treaty of 1818, the United States and Great Britain agree to the forty-ninth parallel as the border between the United States and Canada, from Lake of the Woods (in present-day Minnesota) to the Rocky Mountains. The two countries also agree to the joint occupation of Oregon.

February 1819
In the Adams-Onís Treaty, the United States and Spain establish the forty-second parallel as the boundary between the Oregon country and Spanish landholdings in California and the Southwest. Spain officially relinquishes any claim to Oregon as well as East and West Florida, but retains its hold on Texas.

June 1820
Major Stephen H. Long sets out to explore the Great Plains, which he later labels "the Great American Desert," declaring the treeless prairies unfit for settlement.

1821
The Hudson's Bay Company merges with the North West Company, ending a fierce forty-year rivalry between the two fur-trading firms and establishing the British Hudson's Bay Company as the most organized power in the Oregon country.

February 1821
After eleven years of war, led by revolutionary Agustín de Iturbide, Mexico wins its independence from Spain and takes control of the Southwest.

Fall 1821
While venturing across the southern plains in the fall of 1821, Missouri trader William Becknell meets a company of Mexican soldiers and learns their country is now open to American trade. Becknell hurries to Santa Fe, where his dry goods sell for enormous profits. Returning East with bags of silver pesos, Becknell helps establish the Santa Fe Trail, the 800-mile route between Missouri and New Mexico, as a highway for overland commerce.

March 1821
Moses Austin receives permission to settle 300 American families in Texas. Following his death, his son, Stephen, takes over the colonization effort.

April 1824
Russia and the United States agree to 54°40′ as the border between Russian Alaska and the Oregon country.

July 1825
The first fur trappers' rendezvous is held at Henry's Fork on the Green River. For the next fifteen years, each summer Rocky Mountain trappers meet traders from St. Louis at an appointed site to exchange their years' harvest of furs.

1829
A malaria epidemic, which lasts until 1833, wipes out entire villages of Chinook and Kalapuyan Indians in Oregon's Columbia and Willamette River Valleys. Since the late 1700s, European and American seafarers along the Pacific Coast had introduced diseases such as measles, smallpox, and influenza, which proved deadly to local tribes.

*Mexican traders load their pack
mules for Santa Fe trade.*

*Black Hawk, Sauk
Indian leader*

*Mexican General Antonio López de Santa Anna
surrenders after the Battle of San Jacinto, April 1836.*

1830–1839

May 1830
The U.S. Congress passes the Indian Removal Bill, leading to the forced relocation of tribes in the eastern United States—including the Creeks, Choctaws, Cherokees, and Chickasaws—to lands west of the Mississippi. The Native Americans' former homelands are opened for sale to white settlers.

August 1832
Following the massacre of one hundred fifty Indians at the Battle of Bad Axe, the fifteen-week-long Black Hawk War ends. The surrender of Black Hawk brings to an abrupt close the Sauk and Fox Indians' dispute over an 1804 land treaty with the United States.

September 1834
Methodist Jason Lee arrives in Oregon and builds a school for the Willamette Valley Indians—the first missionary to bring Christianity to Pacific Northwest tribes. Other Methodist, Protestant, and Catholic missionaries soon follow.

September 1836
Dr. Marcus Whitman arrives in Oregon with his wife Narcissa and fellow missionary couple Henry and Eliza Spalding. The Whitmans build a mission on the Walla Walla River for the Cayuse Indians; the Spaldings settle farther east among the Nez Percés.

March 1836
After declaring themselves independent from Mexico, the Texas rebels suffer their first major defeat on March 6, 1836, when Mexican troops slaughter more than one hundred eighty men at the Alamo. On April 21, the Texans have their revenge, defeating the Mexican army in their own camp on the San Jacinto River.

Spring 1841
The first emigrant wagon train, consisting of sixty-nine men, women, and children, leaves Missouri for Oregon guided by mountain men Thomas Fitzpatrick and Joseph Meek. West of the Rocky Mountains at Soda Springs, half of the company decides to head to California.

Spring 1842
With Kit Carson as his guide, Lieutenant John C. Frémont leads a twenty-four man survey of the region between the Missouri River and the Rocky Mountains, his first of three major expeditions in the West. Although Frémont's published reports contain errors and exaggerations (amidst a wealth of valuable geographic descriptions), the explorer becomes a national hero. Thousands of Oregon Trail emigrants use his map as a guide.

Spring 1
The first large group of emigrants to tr the Oregon Trail departs Independe Missouri, with Dr. Marcus Whitman as of their guides. With more than hundred people in about two hun wagons, the company becomes know "the Great Migrati

*Dr. John McLoughlin greets the Whitmans and the Spaldings at
Fort Vancouver, September 1836.*

THE TRIBUNE.

From our Extra of Yesterday Morning.

BY ELECTRIC TELEGRAPH!

CABINET AT WASHINGTON CONVENED
ON SUNDAY MORNING.

50,000 VOLUNTEERS CALLED FOR!

$10,000,000 TO BE RAISED!

Additional and important particulars of War with Mexico!!!

A California gold miner

1840–1849

December 1845
Texas is admitted as the twenty-eighth state in the Union.

May 1846
The U.S. Congress overwhelmingly approves a declaration of war with Mexico after U.S. General Zachary Taylor (under orders from President James Polk) taunts Mexican troops into battle by crossing the Nueces River.

June 1846
In Sonoma, California, a few dozen land-hungry Americans issue a declaration of independence from Mexico, naming their new "country" the Bear Flag Republic. Soon after, they join sides with the United States in the war against Mexico.

June 1846
After more than fifty years of joint occupation, the United States and Great Britain sign a treaty dividing Oregon. A vocal group of American extremists—who popularized the phrase "Fifty-four Forty, or Fight!"—clamor for a war with the British to gain more territory. But, having the war with Mexico to contend with, President Polk skillfully negotiates for a border at the forty-ninth parallel from the Rocky Mountains to the Pacific Ocean.

October 1846
The Donner Party is trapped by early blizzards in the Sierra Nevada. By the following spring, forty-four of the original eighty-nine members have died.

July 1847
Led by Brigham Young, a group of 148 Mormon pioneers arrives at the Salt Lake Valley, having fled Illinois to escape persecution by non-Mormons. Thousands of others wait at Winter Quarters on the Missouri River for directions from the advance party.

November 1847
Increased traffic on the Oregon Trail and a deadly measles epidemic provoke the Cayuse Indians to massacre settlers at the Whitman Mission.

February 1848
The war with Mexico ends with the signing of the Treaty of Guadalupe Hidalgo. Mexico cedes its territories of California and New Mexico (which includes the present-day states of California, New Mexico, Nevada, Utah, and Arizona as well as parts of Colorado and Wyoming) to the United States for fifteen million dollars.

January 1848
Gold is discovered at Sutter's Mill in California, leading to the biggest gold rush in American history.

1

Connecting the Country

The Story of Lewis and Clark

ON AUGUST 12, 1805, Meriwether Lewis knelt and took a drink from the icy waters of the Missouri River near its source in the Rocky Mountains. It was the most satisfying drink he had ever taken. In six days, the army captain and Virginia native would be thirty-one years old, and he was in the middle of the most exciting adventure of his life.

With a small troop of soldiers, backwoodsmen, interpreters, and boatmen, Lewis and his trusted friend, William Clark, had traveled overland farther west than any other Americans. The group had instructions from President Thomas Jefferson to find "the most direct and practicable water [route]" across the North American continent to the Pacific Ocean. President Jefferson hoped the route—if it existed—could be used to transport cargo from the East Coast to the West Coast, thus providing access to the sea otter fur trade in the Pacific and the growing trade with China. If Lewis and Clark were successful, the United States would gain power over its rivals—Great Britain, France, Russia, and Spain.

In a way, the journey had begun almost

Thomas Jefferson, who drafted the Declaration of Independence in 1776, was president of the United States from 1801 to 1809.

twenty years earlier—as a nagging idea in Jefferson's mind. He was curious about the vast, unknown region that stretched west from the Mississippi River to the Rocky Mountains and on to the Pacific Ocean. What little was known to the outside world about this area had come from such explorers as David Thompson and Alexander Mackenzie, who in the 1790s had ventured westward across upper Canada scouting fur-trading opportunities for their employer, the North West Company of Montreal. Several Spanish exploring parties had attempted to reach the Pacific Ocean from New Orleans; but the most successful traveled only sixteen hundred miles up the Missouri River (halfway across the continent) before turning back. Jefferson dreamed of sending a large U.S. expedition through the heart of the continent to be the first to reach the

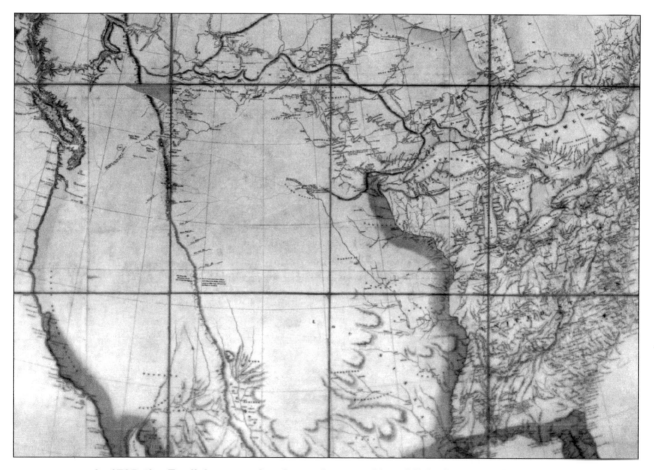

In 1795, the English mapmaker Aaron Arrowsmith published a map of North America based on the overland explorations of David Thompson, a Canadian fur trader. Far to the south, the Spanish had explored the continent's interior by traveling northward through Texas and New Mexico, but thousands of miles remained uncharted. Lewis and Clark's firsthand knowledge, as well as information they acquired from Native Americans, soon allowed cartographers to "fill in" many blank areas on contemporary maps.

Meriwether Lewis, right, was eager to share the responsibilities of the challenging expedition with William Clark. His friend was a skilled engineer and geographer whose outgoing personality complemented Lewis's more introverted nature. While Lewis acted as the businessman and scientific leader, Clark managed the daily operations of the boats and the men.

Pacific. The main obstacle was that Spain claimed Louisiana Territory, the huge wilderness area between the Mississippi River and the Rocky Mountains.

In October 1800, under pressure from the powerful French leader Napoleon Bonaparte, King Charles IV of Spain ceded the great expanse of land to France, which in turn sold it to the United States in 1803. Jefferson, who had become U.S. president in 1801, saw his opportunity. He had already chosen Meriwether Lewis, a young, trustworthy, and adventurous army captain, to lead the expedition.

Lewis had left active military duty to serve as Jefferson's private secretary in 1801. With the expedition in mind, the president encouraged Lewis to learn about the subjects that would make him a competent explorer: mapmaking, botany, natural history, and anthropology. He also sent Lewis to meet with some of the country's leading scientists. In a letter to Dr. Benjamin Rush, a famous Philadelphia physician, Jefferson asked the doctor to "prepare some notes on such particulars as may occur in [Lewis's] journey & which you think should draw his attention and inquiry." Rush complied and later helped Lewis choose medical supplies to take on the journey (including six hundred doses of the doctor's powerful laxatives, popularly known as "Rush's thunderbolts").

In June 1803, Lewis wrote to his long-time friend, William Clark, and asked him to help lead the expedition. A red-haired army lieutenant, Clark had once been Lewis's commanding officer. He was an intelligent, even-tempered man, who had wilderness experience from living on the Kentucky frontier and serving in military campaigns against the Ohio Valley Indians.

Because of bureaucratic reasons, William Clark, left, was never granted the rank of captain that Lewis offered him. (Clark's official rank was second lieutenant.) The two men kept that fact a secret and treated each other as complete equals during the journey.

Washington, June 19th, 1803

Dear Clark:

From the long and uninterrupted friendship and confidence which has subsisted between us I feel no hesitation in making to you the following communication under the fullest impression that it will be held by you inviolably secret.

During the last session of congress a law was passed ... understood by its framers ... to give the sanction of the government to exploring the interior of the continent of North America. ... This enterprise has been confided to me by the President, and in consequence since the beginning of March, I have been engaged in making the necessary preparations for the tour.

... Let me again impress you with the necessity of keeping this matter a perfect secret.

... If therefore there is anything ... in the enterprise, which would induce you to participate with me in its fatigues, its dangers, and its honors, believe me there is no man on earth with whom I should feel equal pleasure in sharing them as with yourself.

Pray write to me on this subject as early as possible.

With sincere and affectionate regard,

Meriwether Lewis

Clarksville, July 17th, 1803

Dear Lewis:

I received by yesterday's Mail your letter of the 19th: the contents of which I received with much pleasure. ... I will cheerfully join you in an "official character" ... and partake of all the Dangers, Difficulties & fatigues ... of such an enterprise. ... My friend, I can assure you that no man lives with whom I would prefer to undertake and share the Difficulties of such a trip than yourself

With every assurance of sincerity,

W. C.

Lewis swore Clark to secrecy in his June 19 letter because the United States was planning to illegally cross land owned by France. Due to slow mail, it took Clark a month to receive Lewis's letter inviting him to help lead the expedition. By the time Clark enthusiastically accepted, their plans could safely be made public, as the United States had purchased Louisiana Territory from France for $15 million—a little more than three cents an acre.

While Lewis waited for Clark's reply, he spent the summer preparing. He stocked up on food, clothing, and medical supplies; a stash of presents to gain the friendship of the Indian tribes they would meet; guns and ammunition to hunt and protect themselves from wild animals or hostile Indians; and scientific instruments, journals, and logs in which to record details on the geography, climate, plants, and animals. Lewis also recruited men who were strong, disciplined, and able to be away from home for a year or more. He wanted men who would not abandon the expedition, despite the isolation, exhaustion, and dangers they were sure to encounter. For transportation, Lewis chose two pirogues (large, flat-bottomed canoes) and a fifty-five-foot-long keelboat with a canvas sail. And finally he spent twenty dollars on a special companion—a large Newfoundland dog.

In late October, the expedition sailed down the Ohio River to its confluence with the Mississippi. On December 12, they stopped near St. Louis for their first winter away from home. The men constructed four sturdy log cabins directly across from the mouth of the Missouri River and called the site Camp Wood. While they waited five long months for spring to melt the ice on the river, they checked and repacked supplies, began keeping scientific records, talked to fur traders who had traveled part way up the Missouri, and visited with the Sauk and Fox Indians.

Lewis was glad to have Clark share the command. While Lewis coordinated their final preparations, the more outgoing Clark trained the men. After the final recruits had been selected, the Corps of Discovery, as the expedition was formally called, consisted of fourteen enlisted soldiers, nine volunteers from Kentucky, two French rivermen, one interpreter, and Clark's slave, York. An additional nine rivermen and seven soldiers would accompany them until the following autumn and then return to St. Louis.

On May 14 at four o'clock in the afternoon, the forty-three-man expedition departed. Two weeks later, they passed the small village of La Charette, the last white settlement on the Missouri River. They had entered the wilderness.

Against a strong current, the corps advanced slowly up the Missouri River, traveling about ten miles a day in the stifling summer heat. Their plan was to ascend the river to its source, and, if possible, transfer their boats to the Columbia River, which they knew emptied into the Pacific Ocean. They rowed, sailed, or pulled the boats from shore with tow ropes, hiking through thick brush and watching for snags in the murky, swift-moving water. It was tiring work, and the men developed blisters on their hands and shoulders from gripping the oars and pulling the ropes. In shallow stretches, they propelled the boats by pushing poles against the river bottom. The mosquitoes were bothersome, and many of

"We are to receive a great reward for this expedition—15 dollars a month and at least 400 acres of first-rate land—and if we make great discoveries, as we expect, the United States has promised to make us great rewards, more than we are promised."

Sergeant John Ordway, Camp Wood, April 8, 1804

the men suffered boils—painful sores caused by extreme fatigue. But gradually they became hardened to the difficult labor.

The land was covered by grasses, and the party found plenty of bear, deer, and elk to hunt. They feasted on the fresh meat, saving their dried foods for times when game was scarce. The farther the men traveled, the less they knew about what lay ahead. Carefully observing the landscape, Lewis and Clark began to see new and strange things. One day, they found a "village of small animals that burrow into the ground." They had heard the French call this animal *petit chien*, or little dog. It was their first encounter with prairie dogs. Lewis described how they caught one "by pouring a great quantity of water in his hole." Then the men tried to dig up another one but, after six feet, found they were "not halfway to his lodge," though they did unearth two frogs and a rattlesnake.

On another occasion, late at night while everyone was asleep, the sergeant of the guard woke Lewis and Clark to see the northern lights dancing in the sky. The aurora borealis glowed in "floating columns, which appeared to approach each other and retreat," Clark wrote with wonderment. He and Lewis logged each discovery in their journals, as President Jefferson had instructed them to record their observations "with great pains & accuracy" and to make extra copies for safekeeping.

All the while, the captains looked for opportunities to arrange meetings with the Native American tribes whose lands they were crossing. The president

During their river travels, Lewis often walked on shore, taking notes and making sketches of the plants, animals, and landscape, while Clark stayed with the boats and plotted their course.

hoped to establish peaceful relationships with the tribes. He instructed Lewis and Clark to inform the Indians that Louisiana Territory now belonged to the United States. Jefferson wanted the Indians to stop trading with U.S. competitors—the French, British, and Spanish.

In late July, Clark tried to arrange a meeting with the Pawnees, but they were away on their annual buffalo hunt. Then, on August 2, a party of the Oto and Missouri nations came to camp. With "every man on his guard and ready for anything," the expedition gave the Indians roasted meat, flour, and meal. "In return," Clark wrote, "they sent us watermelons." During the next couple of days, the two groups exchanged speeches and gifts. With the help of an interpreter, Clark delivered a long speech, "expressive of our journey, the wishes of our government, . . . and directions how they were to conduct themselves." After distributing medals, clothing, a flag, a canister of gunpowder, and a bottle of whiskey to the chiefs, Lewis shot off the party's powerful air gun. The weapon's loud popping noise and straight shot "astonished" the Indians.

The corps also had peaceful meetings with the Arikaras, who were fascinated with York. The Arikaras had never seen a black man and wished to examine him "from top to toe." To impress them, York "carried on the joke and made himself more terrible than we wished him to do," Clark wrote. For the Arikaras and many other tribes, the dark-skinned, six-foot-tall York was an exotic and powerful presence. On later occasions,

Inquiries Relative to the Indians of Louisiana

- At what age do both Sexes usually marry?
- What time do they generally consume in Sleep?
- What is the nature of their baths, and at what time of the day do they generally use them?
- What are the Vices most common among the Indians?
- Do they use animal sacrifices in their Worship?
- How do they dispose of their dead?
- Do they Mourn for their deceased friends?
- From what quarter of the earth did they emigrate as related to them by their ancestors?
- Do they have any domestic animals?
- How do they pursue, and how take their game?
- What is the ceremony of declaring war, and making peace?
- Do they burn and torture their prisoners?
- Do they ever dance?
- Have they any music?

Wanting to learn as much as possible about the western Indian tribes, President Jefferson had given Lewis and Clark a long and detailed list of questions to guide them.

Lewis and Clark distributed Peace and Friendship Medals to Indian chiefs to help establish peaceful relations. Metal coins were highly valued by Native Americans, and the recipients proudly wore the gifts on ribbons or chains strung around their necks. The medals also functioned as an invitation and "passport" for the chiefs to visit the United States.

among the Mandan and Nez Percé Indians, York patiently let the most curious men lick a finger and try to rub off his color.

But not all encounters with Indians would proceed so peacefully. At the end of September, the expedition had a scare with the Teton Sioux, who were well-supplied with guns obtained from trading with the British. The Tetons demanded more and more gifts and then insisted that the expedition pay a fee—a pirogue loaded with goods—for the right to continue upriver. Lewis and Clark steadfastly refused. After a few tense days during which the men were constantly on guard, the expedition managed to forge on. An exhausted Clark wrote, "I am very unwell for want of sleep."

William Clark used this elkskin-bound journal (one of many) to record the expedition's daily progress. Keeping careful records while traveling through the wild could be difficult. On July 26, 1804, Clark wrote, "The wind blustering and hard from the south all day in such a manner that I could not complete my plan in the tent. The boat rolled in such a manner that I could do nothing in that, and was compelled to go to the woods and combat the mosquitoes."

As the days grew colder and winter approached, the corps hurried to the site of the Mandan Indian villages where they hoped to build a camp. They had traveled sixteen hundred miles since the previous winter, but they still had half a continent to go.

The hospitable Mandans agreed to let the expedition build a wood fortress on the bank of the river across from one of their villages. For the next five months, during heavy snows and sub-zero temperatures, the men passed the time hunting, trading, and socializing with the Mandans and neighboring Hidatsa tribes. One of the rivermen, Pierre Cruzatte, often played his fiddle in the evenings so the men could dance jigs and square dances. The captains made copies of their journals, and Clark spent hours creating new maps using their geographical notes and information from the Native Americans. He called the process "connecting the country," for indeed, he was filling in details on the vast uncharted area of the continent.

As planned, with the arrival of spring, Lewis and Clark sent a small

In August 1805, Lewis and Clark met a group of friendly Indians at Ross's Hole (in present-day Montana). During their travels, the expedition's talented interpreter, George Drouillard, helped them communicate with the tribes they met—mainly through sign language. Though Lewis acknowledged the language was "imperfect and liable to error," he also wrote that "the strong parts of the ideas are seldom mistaken."

party downstream in the keelboat to return to St. Louis with their journal copies, weather tables and scientific records, letters, plant and animal specimens such as grasses, leaves, seeds, and animal hides, and even some live animals—a prairie dog and four magpies.

Lewis and Clark hired three white traders as interpreters and guides for the journey west, including a French-Canadian named Toussaint Charbonneau. Charbonneau convinced them to let him bring his young wife, a teenaged Shoshone girl named Sacajawea who had been captured by a Hidatsa war party and then sold to him. The captains were reluctant to bring a woman on the journey, especially one who had just given birth to a baby that February; but they relented when they realized Sacajawea might be able to help them acquire horses from the Shoshones to carry the corps across the steep passes of the Rocky Mountains. Sacajawea proved helpful in other, unexpected ways. She served as a guide and interpreter when the expedition reached the lands where she had grown up, and her presence helped convince other Native American

tribes that the Corps of Discovery was a peaceful expedition: A war party wouldn't travel with a woman and a baby.

On the windy spring day of April 7, the expedition left the Mandan villages. The men set a steady pace, rowing and pulling the pirogues. As the frosty spring mornings and occasional snow flurries gave way to warm summer days, the grassy prairies became drier and trees more scarce. They continued to discover animals and plants they had never seen before, such as bighorn sheep and coyotes. And finally they encountered the grizzly bear, of which they had heard magnificent stories from the Native Americans.

"The Indians give a very formidable account of the strength and ferocity of this animal, which they never dare to attack but in parties of six, eight, or ten persons," Lewis wrote on April 13, 1805. Still, his men were anxious to test their own hunting prowess. On April 29, after being chased "seventy or eighty yards" by a bear while walking on shore, Lewis remarked, "It is astonishing to see the wounds they will bear before they can be put to death," although he felt that "in the hands of skillful riflemen, [grizzly bears] are by no means as formidable or dangerous as they have been presented."

A week later, Lewis wrote, "Captain Clark and Drouillard killed the largest brown bear this evening which we have yet seen." With "five balls through his lungs and five others in various parts," it took twenty minutes for the animal to die. He "swam more than half the distance across the river, [and] made the most tremendous roaring from the moment he was shot." After a few more encounters hunting grizzlies—including one where a member of the expedition was chased for almost a mile by a wounded bear—the men learned not to provoke the animals. On May 11, Lewis admitted that the grizzly bears "rather intimidate us all" and confessed he would rather "fight two Indians than one bear."

On May 26, the expedition sighted the Rocky Mountains. They were excited to finally have come upon the great range but knew that crossing the snowy peaks would be their most difficult test yet. The river became more treacherous, and the men were forced to wade as deep as their armpits in the icy water to guide the canoes around rocky obstructions. The river bottom was so muddy and slippery that they went barefoot to secure their footing, and sharp rocks cut their feet. Their labor was "incredibly painful and great," Lewis wrote.

Soon they reached the Great Falls of the Missouri, a beautiful but dangerous series of waterfalls—"jets of sparkling foam to the height of fifteen or twenty feet." Realizing they would have to abandon river travel and continue overland, Lewis and Clark had the men hide one of their canoes and some supplies under a pile of brush, planning to recover them on the trip home. Then they cut down cottonwood trees and built crude wagons to carry the remaining canoes. The trip over the steep, mountainous terrain was made even more difficult by bruising hailstorms and swarms of mosquitoes. It took them almost a month to cover just sixteen miles.

At last, they reached a point where they could continue upriver by canoe. Sacajawea, who had begun to recognize familiar terrain from her

---

Hungry Creek and Bad-Humored Island

Lewis and Clark recorded each new landmark, large or small, in their journals and on the maps they were creating. Sometimes they adopted names they heard from the Native Americans and trappers. But often they had to think of new names, so they named rivers after the president, the secretary of state, and the secretary of treasury. They even called one stream the Judith, for Clark's future wife, Judith Hancock. Many times, they created names that reflected the type of day they had had or sites they had seen. They called one stream Fourth of July 1804 Creek because they camped there on Independence Day and named a nearby lake Gosling Lake because they had seen "great numbers of goslings . . . which were nearly grown." There was also Hungry Creek—"at that place we had nothing to eat," Onion Creek—"from the quantity of wild onions which grow . . . on its borders," Charbonneau's Creek—"after our interpreter," and even Bad-Humored Island—"as we were in a bad humor [that day]."

Sometimes the event was more serious, such as when Sergeant Charles Floyd suffered an appendicitis attack. On August 19, 1804, Clark recorded, "Sergeant Floyd is taken very bad all at once with a bilious colic. We attempt to relieve him without much success." By the next day, Floyd was "as bad as he can be," Clark reported, "No pulse, and nothing will stay a moment on his stomach or bowels." Floyd died that day, and the expedition sadly forged on, but not before holding a solemn funeral and naming a small river after the well-liked man. There they erected a cedar post that read:

Sergeant C. Floyd
died here
20th of August
1804

And so the landscape took on names that made it seem more familiar and helped them remember what had happened at each point along the way. Amazingly, Floyd was the only member of the expedition to die.

childhood, helped guide them. Lewis and Clark were eager to find the Shoshone Indians. They hoped the Shoshones would help them plan a route over the uncharted mountains and trade them horses. On August 13, to Lewis's joy, the expedition came upon a group of Indians—two women, a man, and some dogs—who reluctantly led the white strangers to their camp.

Here the expedition had an amazing turn of luck: the Shoshone chief, Cameâhwait, was Sacajawea's long-lost brother. After a warm reunion, the Shoshones shared what food they could spare—some salmon and camas roots—and warned the expedition that there was no easy river

Carrying her infant son, Jean Baptiste, on her back, in August 1805, Sacajawea had an emotional reunion with her tribe, the Shoshones. After serving as an interpreter while Lewis and Clark traded with the Shoshones for horses, Sacajawea continued on the journey with the explorers. She and her husband, Toussaint Charbonneau, finally bade the Americans good-bye after returning to the Mandan Indian villages where they had first joined the expedition more than a year earlier.

route across the mountains to the Columbia River. The rapids were un-navigable and banked by sheer cliffs, along which travel was impossible. Lewis and Clark's crew stashed what goods they could no longer carry and stored their remaining canoes by filling them with heavy rocks and sinking them in the chilly river water. They hoped this storage method would preserve the boats better than if they were left out in the winter snows, exposed to the elements and in danger of being stolen. After purchasing horses from the tribe, the expedition continued on with a Shoshone guide named Old Toby.

Although it was only early September, snow was already beginning to fall. Slowly they made their way over mountain paths so steep and narrow that some of the horses lost their footing and fell to their death. Game was scarce and the men became sick from exhaustion and hunger. They were forced to eat some of the horses. By mid-October, as they wound their way down through the foothills of the Rockies, the expedition met a friendly Nez Percé tribe who offered food and good news. From where they were, it was possible to travel by river to the ocean. A chief named Twisted Hair drew a map on a piece of white elkskin, and Lewis and Clark arranged to leave their horses with him until their return journey the next spring. Crafting five new canoes from trees, they set off along the Clearwater and Snake Rivers to the Columbia. Desperately short of provisions, they resorted to eating dogs purchased from tribes along the way.

Traveling swiftly downriver, in the second week of November, Lewis

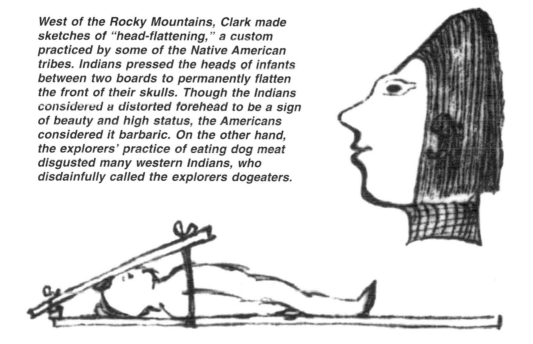

West of the Rocky Mountains, Clark made sketches of "head-flattening," a custom practiced by some of the Native American tribes. Indians pressed the heads of infants between two boards to permanently flatten the front of their skulls. Though the Indians considered a distorted forehead to be a sign of beauty and high status, the Americans considered it barbaric. On the other hand, the explorers' practice of eating dog meat disgusted many western Indians, who disdainfully called the explorers dogeaters.

The members of the Corps of Discovery spent a miserable winter at Fort Clatsop. Their lodging became infested with fleas, and the constantly gray, rainy weather caused their clothing to mildew and their food to spoil.

and Clark's expedition reached the Pacific Ocean. After two years and more than four thousand miles, they could trek no farther west. Near the coast, they built their third winter camp—a pine stockade called Fort Clatsop after a local Indian tribe. The stockade had seven rooms—one for Lewis and Clark, one for Charbonneau's family, two for supplies, and three for the rest of the men to crowd into.

The almost constant winter rains drenched the men and made them wish for the snowy plains. The coastal Indians were civil and helpful, but drove a hard bargain when trading, and occasionally stole from them. These Indians had been trading sea otter furs with European trading ships for more than ten years—some even wore sailors' jackets. The Indians saw no reason to give the white men who had arrived by land special treatment, and they couldn't understand why Lewis and Clark wouldn't buy any furs. Compared to the inland tribes, who had been awestruck at their air gun and trinkets and excited to establish trading ties, the coastal Indians seemed "assuming and disagreeable."

The corps passed the gloomy winter months repairing their equipment, hunting, drying meat for the return journey, boiling sea water to obtain salt for preserving food, and sewing new clothes of elkskin. Again the captains prepared extensive notes on the number and location of the Indian tribes as well as their customs and appearances. They described more plant species the Sitka spruce, grand fir, western white pine, and Oregon grape—and new animals, too—the blacktailed deer, Oregon bobcat, steelhead trout, and whistling swan.

At Christmas, the men exchanged makeshift gifts. Lewis and Clark gave tobacco and silk scarves, and Clark recorded that Sacajawea gave him two dozen white

> Washington, U.S. of America. July 4, 1803
> To Capt. Meriwether Lewis
>
> Dear Sir,
>
> In the journey which you are about to undertake, ... it is to be expected that you will encounter considerable dangers.... Should you escape those dangers and reach the Pacific Ocean, you may find it imprudent to hazard a return the same way and be forced to seek a passage round by sea in such vessels as you may find on the Western coast. But you will be without money, without clothes, & other necessaries, as a sufficient supply cannot be carried with you from hence. Your resource in that case can only be in the credit of the United States, for which purpose I hereby authorize you to draw on the Secretaries of State, of the Treasury, of War, & of the Navy ... for the purpose of obtaining money or necessaries for yourself & your men. ... I also ask of the consuls, agents, merchants, & citizens of any nation with which we have intercourse or amity to furnish you with those supplies which your necessities may call for. ... And to give more entire satisfaction & confidence to those who may be disposed to aid you, I, Thomas Jefferson, President of the United States of America, have written this letter of general credit for you ... and signed it with my name.
>
> Thomas Jefferson

Jefferson wrote Lewis a letter of credit to be used to bargain for sea passage home if the explorers met a trading ship after arriving at the Pacific Coast. Although an American ship, the Lydia, *spent the winter along the coast, Lewis and Clark failed to sight the vessel from Fort Clatsop and had to return home overland.*

After returning home, Lewis posed for this portrait wearing a cape that Cameâhwait, chief of the Shoshones, had given him. Three years later, while governor of Louisiana Territory, Lewis died of gunshot wounds inflicted late at night at an inn in Tennessee. Though it was never proven, most believe he committed suicide. William Clark lived until 1838 and served a long career as superintendent of Indian Affairs for the federal government. About 1832, Clark freed his slave, York.

weasel tails. But Christmas dinner consisted of "poor elk, so much spoiled that [they] ate it through mere necessity, some spoiled pounded fish, and a few roots." For New Year's Day, they fired a rifle salute, but found little other means of celebrating the holiday.

Finally, on March 23, they loaded their canoes and began the homeward journey. The men were "elated with the idea of moving on toward their friends and country," Lewis later reported. But they had left too early. When they reached the Rocky Mountains in mid-June, they were forced to wait for more snow to melt. The frustrated Lewis wrote in his journal, "This is the first time . . . we have ever been compelled to retreat." The party was "a good deal dejected."

They retrieved their horses from Chief Twisted Hair on June 24, and continued over now-familiar terrain. In early July, the corps divided into two groups, with Clark venturing southeast to explore the Yellowstone River and Lewis's group heading along the Marias River to the north. The two parties joined again at the meeting of the Yellowstone and Missouri Rivers and crossed the plains together late in the summer.

By September, they were nearing civilization. They ran into occasional fur traders from St. Louis, and, on September 20, saw "some cows on the bank, which . . . caused a shout to be raised for joy." Later that afternoon, the corps reached the small town of La Charette. On shore, "every person . . . seemed to express great pleasure at our return," Clark wrote. "They informed us that we were supposed to have been lost long since."

At a celebration dinner in a St. Louis tavern, Lewis and Clark were congratulated with one toast after another. Then the Corps of Discovery was disbanded. Although they had not found the fabled Northwest Passage—a navigable water route from the Atlantic Ocean to the Pacific Ocean—they had returned with an incredible wealth of information. They had studied more than 40 Indian tribes, discovered 122 new animals, and described 178 new types of plants. No longer was the continent's western half a mysterious void. With meticulous notes and mapmaking, Lewis and Clark had succeeded in "connecting the country."

As Jefferson had hoped, Lewis and Clark's exploration soon helped the United States compete against Great Britain, Spain, and Russia for the territory west of the Rockies. Later adventurers would find more easily crossed mountain passes and trails, but Lewis and Clark's journey is still remembered as the most amazing expedition in all of American history. ◑

2

Furs and Adventure

Trapping in the Rocky Mountains

WHEN LEWIS AND CLARK RETURNED to St. Louis, word of their findings spread like wildfire. In the frontier town's streets, shops, boatyards, and saloons, conversations buzzed with details of the expedition's adventures. One word, in particular, created a blaze of desire in fortune-hunting businessmen: beaver!

Nicknamed "soft gold," beaver furs brought top prices in America and Europe because of the widespread popularity of the beaver felt hat. For two hundred years, British, Spanish, and French fur traders had explored the Ohio and Mississippi River Valleys and the area around the Great Lakes looking for pelts to meet this demand. They bartered for beaver, fox, weasel, and river otter skins with Native Americans, who were eager for their steel knives, iron hatchets, and fishhooks. However, in 1806 when Lewis and Clark returned, few white men had penetrated the unmapped, inner regions of the continent. Lewis and Clark's reports of mountain streams teeming with long, silky-haired beaver inspired many to venture west into Louisiana Territory.

In the cities of the East Coast and Europe, no fashionable man's wardrobe was complete without a gleaming top hat made of beaver fur.

One member of the Lewis and Clark expedition, Private John Colter, was immediately drawn to the fur trade. On the return journey from the Pacific, Colter left the expedition to join two Illinois hunters who hired him as a guide. Together, the three men paddled up the snag-filled Missouri in search of beaver. The next year, Colter was hired by Manuel Lisa, a Spanish-American trader from St. Louis. As part of a forty-two-man expedition, Colter again headed toward the distant Rocky Mountains. At the junction of the Bighorn and Yellowstone Rivers, the men built a trading fort on the newly acquired U.S. territory as a base for their activities.

After they finished the fort, Colter rode on horseback deeper into the mountains looking for Native Americans interested in trading. Soon after he met a group of Flathead Indians, he found himself caught in a skirmish between the Flatheads and a rival group of Blackfeet. Even after being injured in the leg, Colter continued to fire his musket at the Blackfeet from a hiding place in the brush. With the help of Colter and three hundred

The Blackfoot Indians were skilled horsemen and buffalo hunters as well as fierce warriors.

About 9 o'clock a.m., we were arouse[d] by an alarm of "Indians." We ran to our horses [and] succeeded in driving them into Camp where we caught all but 6, which escaped into the Prairie. In the meantime, the Indians appeared before our camp to the number of 60, of which 15 or 20 were mounted on horseback & the remainder on foot—all being entirely naked, armed with fusees, bows, arrows, etc. They immediately caught the horses which had escaped from us and commenced riding to and fro within gunshot of our Camp with all the speed their horses were capable of producing, without shooting a single gun for about 20 minutes, brandishing their war weapons, and yelling at the top of their voices. Some had Scalps suspended on small poles, which they waved in the air.

Osborne Russell, trapper, at Pierre's Hole (a western valley of the Rocky Mountains), June 28, 1835

Crow Indians who rode in to join the fight, the Flatheads succeeded in chasing the Blackfeet away. Little did Colter know, as he painfully made his way back to the fort, that he was helping to upset the delicate relations among the Native American tribes.

For decades, the Blackfoot Indians, who lived between the Missouri and Saskatchewan Rivers, had traded with the French and British, acquiring guns and ammunition. They also prevented the white traders from reaching the tribes farther west, thus forcing the traders to rely on the Blackfeet for furs and keeping them more powerfully armed than their enemies.

However, by the early 1800s, as fur companies pushed farther into the wilderness, newcomers began trapping on Blackfoot land. Some companies enlisted the Crow Indians as middlemen to trade with the Flathead and Snake tribes to the west. Soon most of the Blackfeet's enemies were supplied with guns, and Blackfoot lands were infiltrated by white men who no longer paid them for the furs they gathered. The Blackfeet retaliated. With increasing frequency, they murdered and scalped traders and stole their horses and equipment.

After Colter's wounds healed, he boldly returned to trapping, but the Blackfeet had not forgotten the white man who had fought with their enemy. In 1808, near the Jefferson River, Colter and a companion were caught by the Blackfeet. They killed Colter's partner and decided to teach the hated trapper a lesson. They stripped Colter naked and gave him a running head start. Barefoot, he set off at breakneck speed across the rocky, cactus-covered plain. Young warriors chased him, but Colter managed to outrun all but one. When the young brave reached him,

Colter spun around and killed the Indian with his own spear. Colter then leaped into a nearby river and hid under a tangle of driftwood. The other warriors soon caught up and furiously searched for him. Breathing from a small pocket of air under the logs and branches, Colter hid in the frigid water until dark. Then, still naked and with his feet pricked and bloodied by cactus needles, he limped slowly toward the fort. Eating roots to stay alive, he made it back in just over a week.

As Colter and others discovered, the upper Missouri River basin had

---

A Close Escape

One year in late August, a mountain man named Osborne Russell was setting traps near the Yellowstone River, when the following episode occurred. In his autobiography, Russell wrote this account.

"After eating . . . I arose and kindled a fire, filled my tobacco pipe, and sat down to smoke. My comrade, whose name was White, was still sleeping. Presently I cast my eyes towards the horses which were feeding in the Valley and discovered the heads of some Indians who were . . . within thirty steps of me. I jumped to my rifle and aroused White. . . . We cocked our rifles and started . . . into the woods which seemed to be completely filled with Blackfeet who rent the air with their horrid yells. On presenting our rifles they opened a space about twenty feet wide through which we plunged. About the fourth jump, an arrow struck White on the right hip joint. I hastily told him to pull it out and [as] I spoke, another arrow struck me in the same place, but they did not retard our progress. At length, another arrow striking through my right leg above the knee benumbed the flesh so that I fell with my breast across a log. The Indian who shot me was within eight feet and made a spring towards me with his uplifted battle ax: I made a leap and avoided the blow and kept hopping from log to log through a shower of arrows which flew around us like hail, lodging in the pines and logs. . . . We then ran and hopped about fifty yards further. . . . About twenty [Blackfeet] passed by us within fifteen feet without casting a glance towards us. . . . They were all well armed. . . . We sat still until the rustling among the bushes had died away then . . . White asked in a whisper how far it was to the lake. I replied about a quarter of a mile. I was nearly faint from the loss of blood and the want of water. . . . We hobbled along . . . until we reached the bank of the lake [and continued] for a mile and a half when it grew dark and we stopped. We could still hear the shouting of the [Indians]."

Eventually, Russell and White made it to a British trading fort, more than sixty-five miles away. With the generosity of the fort's employees, Russell rested and took care of his wounds, bathing them in salt water and applying a medicinal salve. Always the trapper, within ten days he was "again setting traps for Beaver."

become far too dangerous for profitable beaver trading. Each year, fur companies lost employees and pack horses loaded with goods to brutal attacks by the Blackfoot Indians and other tribes, such as the Sioux, Arikaras, and Assiniboins, who were also angered by white trappers moving into their lands.

One perceptive man from St. Louis, a former real estate speculator named William Henry Ashley, began to rethink the way the fur business was run. At the time, most companies built forts in the wilderness and encouraged Native Americans to bring pelts there to trade. The fixed posts were difficult to defend, and the Indians who came to them didn't bring enough furs to satisfy the profit-minded businessmen. In addition, forts had to be constantly restocked by keelboats and pack trains, which were ransacked by tribes who found stealing the white man's goods to be much easier than trading.

On February 13, 1822, Ashley placed an advertisement in the St. Louis *Missouri Gazette and Public Advertiser*. He called for one hundred "enterprising young men" to ascend the Missouri to its source and be employed in the mountain wilderness for as long as three years. Ashley and his partner, Andrew Henry, did not intend to rely entirely on Indians for furs. Instead, they would also hire white trappers to comb the mountains independently for beaver. They would pay the men according to the number and quality of pelts they gathered, thereby giving the men incentive to scour streams and rivers far and wide.

Ashley's ad proved irresistible to men from many walks of life. Among the first to respond were Mike Fink, a fifty-two-year-old boatman who was bored with river life; Jedediah Smith, a devout but ambitious twenty-three-year-old from New Hampshire, who never traveled without his Bible; and James Beckwourth, the son of a white Virginia planter and a black slave, who abandoned his apprenticeship with a quarrelsome St. Louis blacksmith. All of the men who were hired had an unquenchable taste for adventure.

The first year, Ashley and Henry sent small groups to the

TO
Enterprising Young Men.

THE subscriber wishes to engage ONE HUN- DRED MEN to ascend the river Missouri to its source, there to be employed for one, two, or three years. —For particulars, enquire of Major Andrew Henry, near the Lead Mines, in the County of Washington, (who will ascend with and command the party) or to the subscriber at St. Louis.

Wm. H. Ashley.

February 13

The men who responded to Ashley's advertisement were eager to take on the challenge of the western wilderness. Americans thought of Louisiana Territory as an untamed land—far outside the bounds of civilization—that was filled with ferocious, wild animals and hostile Indians.

For the many risks a trapper took, he earned a lifestyle of independence and self-sufficiency, breaking trails where no white men had gone before. After a year or two in the mountains, a man was judged not by the color of his skin or his family's social status but by his ability to survive and to trap large numbers of furs. Despite the hair-raising stories, the fur trade continued to lure adventuresome men into its ranks.

beaver-hunting regions of the upper Missouri, but a brutal battle with the Arikara Indians and continued attacks by the Blackfeet convinced them to concentrate on the more remote central Rocky Mountains. Instead of trying to build and manage a trading fort in the faraway Rockies, Ashley improvised again. He decided that once a year, during the summer—when overland travel was easiest and hunting for beaver the least profitable because of the animal's thin, warm-weather coat—he would haul a well-defended caravan of supplies from St. Louis and meet the trappers at a

The Rise and Fall of Astoria

While American fur traders scrambled for the Rocky Mountains, one New York fur merchant was drawn to the Pacific Northwest. John Jacob Astor saw the opportunity to trade for valuable sea otter pelts, as well as to tap the riches of the inland beaver trade via the Columbia River and its tributaries. With an outpost at the mouth of the Columbia (near where Lewis and Clark had camped for the winter), he could ship the pelts across the Pacific to China and trade for silks and porcelain dishware, which he could sell for enormous profits back in America.

In 1810, envisioning great riches, Astor sent two expeditions to the Northwest to establish operations for his new venture— the Pacific Fur Company. Thirty-three young men sailed from New York on the *Tonquin*, while a second, larger group set off for Oregon on horseback. After seven months at sea, in late March of 1811, the *Tonquin* neared the Columbia River on the tree-lined coast of Oregon. Rather than wait for calm seas to cross the river's mouth, the ship's impatient captain, Jonathan Thorn, sailed straight into the treacherous waters; eight men died in the churning tides.

The captain proved to be irresponsible in many instances, including one in which he lost his temper during a trade meeting and struck an Indian chief in the face with an otter pelt. But his last misjudgment proved fatal. Having left a group of men to build the fort at Astoria, as the post was called, Thorn sailed the *Tonquin* north to

trade. Off Vancouver Island, he ignored Astor's advice never to let more than a few Indians on board at a time. A group of Indians with knives and clubs hidden under the furs they carried attacked Thorn's outnumbered crew. The following day, rather than surrender, one of the surviving crew members snuck into the ship's hold and lit off four and a half tons of gunpowder—blowing himself, the Indians, and the *Tonquin* to smithereens.

Meanwhile, Astor's overland party had troubles of its own. Intimidated by hostile Indians, the group changed its course, abandoning the land route and horses for handmade canoes and a death-defying ride down the Snake River. They survived some of the most dangerous rapids in North America but soon ran so low on food they had to boil their moccasins to make broth.

In January 1812, the overland party finally straggled into Astoria. Without the *Tonquin*, the company had no way to resupply the fort. The desperate traders sent a return party overland to New York. Led by Robert Stuart, a twenty-seven-year-old Scotsman, the seven men took a more

John Jacob Astor's briefly occupied post in the Oregon country helped establish a U.S. claim to the territory.

southerly route than the original party and found a much easier way across the Rocky Mountains. This important discovery—a low, gently graded pass across the rugged Continental Divide—came to be known as South Pass. However, to keep competing fur companies from using it, Astor kept the discovery quiet. (It wasn't until mountain man Jedediah Smith rediscovered the crossing in 1824 that it became known to other Americans and used as a crucial part of the Oregon Trail.)

Still, the Astorians' troubles were far from over. No sooner had they established their remote fort than David Thompson, an explorer for the North West Company of Montreal, arrived. He was disappointed to find the Americans had beat him, but the presence of the Astorians didn't deter the competitive Canadian company. Since the 1790s, they had branched west from Montreal, expanding their fur-trading network to the Pacific Northwest. But, competition between the fur traders ended abruptly with the outbreak of the War of 1812. News of conflict between the United States and Great Britain reached Astoria in early 1813. Astor's men were forced to sell the fort to the North West Company at a great financial loss, and on November 30, a British warship arrived and took possession of it.

Although his property was eventually returned, Astor's Pacific Northwest fur ambitions had failed. While the British and Canadians expanded into the Oregon country, the determined businessman went on to monopolize the American fur trade in the Great Lakes, Missouri River, and Rocky Mountain regions with another venture—the American Fur Company. Astor retired from the fur trade in 1834, before the collapse in beaver prices, and by the time he died in 1848, he was the wealthiest man in America.

A typical steel beaver trap weighed a hefty five pounds or more.

designated place. There they could bring their year's catch to sell and purchase supplies for the next season. This temporary wilderness market came to be called a rendez-vous. And, just as Ashley had hoped, it made him a very rich man.

Within a few years, several hundred hardy trappers had trekked westward on horseback to the high, unmapped valleys of the Rockies. The "mountain men," as they came to be known, worked by themselves or in small groups. Rising before daybreak to set their steel-jawed traps in frigid mountain streams, they waded through the water to cover their scent from the wary beavers. At sunset, they checked the traps. If they were lucky and had chosen their sites well, the men would have hides to clean and skin when they gathered around the campfire that night. The trappers stretched the skins on circular hoops made of tree branches, which they would set in the sun for a few days to dry. Then, rolling the skins fur side in, they packed them in bundles until they could be sold or traded.

For meals, mountain men ate roasted buf-falo meat, boiled beaver tails, rabbit, elk, and fish. When game was scarce and their dried foods ran out, they resorted to eating plant roots, locusts, and snails, or sometimes even their pack horses. For clothing, they

Trapper Jim Bridger was renowned for his mapping skills. With a piece of animal skin and some charcoal, he could accurately draw the paths of his widespread travels. Bridger is believed to have been the first white man to discover the Great Salt Lake. (When the grizzled trapper tasted the salty water, he mistook it for part of the Pacific Ocean.) During his long career in the West, Bridger outlived three Native American wives, became an army scout and wagon train guide, and set up a fort and trading post on the Oregon Trail.

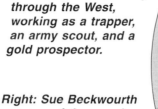

Left: After becoming a mountain man, James Beckwourth spent a number of years with the Crow Indians, who thought he had been stolen by a war party from them when he was a baby. At first, Beckwourth's Crow name was Morning Star, but after he led a few successful—and deadly—raids against the Blackfeet, his name was changed to "Bloody Arm." Beckwourth went on to travel extensively through the West, working as a trapper, an army scout, and a gold prospector.

Right: Sue Beckwourth was one of the roaming trapper's many Native American wives.

wore the same buckskin leggings, shirt, and moccasins for months on end.

Riding relaxed in their saddles, with sun-darkened skin, long hair, and worn leather clothing, many Rocky Mountain trappers were mistaken for Indians. And soon enough, some felt they had more in common with Native Americans than with the people back "home." Many paired up with Indian women for companionship and discovered that their new wives were more skilled at cleaning and drying skins than they were. In addition, the women knew the best ways to find and prepare food in the mountainous terrain. Fights between trappers and Indians still occurred, but the incidents were more isolated and personal than the widespread aggressions that had developed among the upper Missouri tribes.

When the ice on the streams grew too thick to break and trapping became impossible, mountain men holed up for the winter in skin lodges, small log cabins, or the villages of friendly Indian tribes. During the short, dark days, when the ground was blanketed with snow, they cleaned and repaired their guns and equipment or mended their clothing. Some took the time to have a friend teach them how to read. But, as soon as the spring ice began to break, they were hard at work again.

Late in the spring of 1825, William Ashley's Rocky Mountain Fur Company hosted the first rendezvous on the Green River. It was a rousing event, with horse races, wrestling matches, shooting contests, card games, and fistfights. Happy to have company after a year of near solitude, the trappers drank, sang, hollered, and danced until all hours of

"We all had snug lodges made of dressed Buffalo skins in the center of which we built a fire and generally comprised about six men to the lodge. The long winter evenings were passed away by collecting in some of the most spacious lodges and entering into debates . . . or spinning long yarns until midnight in perfect good humor."

Osborne Russell, at a winter camp near the Yellowstone River, 1836–1837

Along with the American trappers, hundreds of Native Americans also attended the annual rendezvous. The Indians traded furs, horses, and dried meat for kettles, guns, bright cloth, and other goods from St. Louis, and participated in horse races and shooting contests.

the night. Telling tall tales by the campfire, each man tried to convince the others that he was the strongest, smartest, and wittiest of all.

Each year afterward, trappers straggled in to the appointed rendez-vous site, their pack animals loaded with furs, and eagerly watched the horizon for the dust clouds of the approaching St. Louis caravan. When the long mule train appeared, cheers arose and the festivities went into high gear. Now the trappers could trade in their furs and fill their saddle-bags with tobacco, gunpowder, coffee, sugar, and flour, and purchase new guns, knives, and traps. Several companies competed for the trap-pers' furs—including the Rocky Mountain Fur Company and John Jacob

"After supper . . . we spread the Bull skin down in the mud in the driest place we could find and laid down upon it. Our fire was immediately put out by the rain and all was . . . darkness. We lay tolerably comfortable whilst the skin . . . remained above the surface, but the mud being soft, the weight of our bodies sunk it by degrees below the water level, which ran under us on the skin. . . . We concluded it was best to lie still and keep the water warm that was about us, for if we stirred we let in the cold water, and if we removed our bed we were more likely to find a worse instead of a better place as it rained very hard all night. At daylight, we arose . . . and left as fast as our legs would carry us through the mud and water, and after traveling about twelve miles . . . we stopped and killed a bull and took breakfast."

Osborne Russell

Astor's American Fur Company—and all of them charged the trappers exorbitant prices for the goods from St. Louis. Men who had been in the mountains for a few years had no way of comparing prices and no means of dealing with anyone else. Thus, the investors in the East grew rich, while many of the mountain men spent their entire year's earnings on overpriced goods, gambling, and watered-down alcohol before they had even left the rendezvous.

In many ways, the life of a trapper was not easy. He was in danger of being attacked by wild animals and had to guard against marauding Indians. To set his traps, he frequently crossed icy cold, swift-flowing mountain streams, and he had to avoid avalanches in the winter and floods in the spring and fall. If he fell ill or was wounded, he had to doctor himself or find a friend to help. A mountain man withstood everything from blizzards and driving rains to blazing sunshine, with only animal skins and temporary shelters to protect himself.

This is the only known portrait of Jedediah Smith, who in 1825 captured the all-time record for the number of beaver pelts trapped in one year: 688. Smith had other, more gruesome, claims to fame. In addition to several deadly Indian attacks, he survived a terrible mauling by a grizzly bear, after which his companions had to sew his ripped scalp and ear back on. In May 1831, en route to Santa Fe to trade with the Mexicans, he was surrounded by Comanche Indians at a water hole and killed.

Many of the daring and competitive men traveled thousands of miles each year, looking for new beaver streams or trying to find an easier path across a troublesome mountain range. They roamed to satisfy their curiosity, always wanting to see what was beyond the next ridge. Or sometimes they roamed simply because it was in their blood.

This adventuresome spirit led to a rash of discoveries and trailblazing from the deserts of the Southwest to the forests of the Oregon country. In 1824, Jedediah Smith, one of the original men hired by William Ashley, rediscovered South Pass, the gap in the Rockies that would later be used by thousands of emigrants on the Oregon Trail. (Fourteen years earlier, a group from Astoria had traveled east across the pass en route to Boston, but their discovery was largely forgotten until Smith happened upon the pass.)

Two years later, Smith led the first overland group of Americans to California, which he identified as "the country southwest of the Great Salt Lake [and] west of the Rocky Mountains." By the end of the trip, the men had "but one horse and one mule remaining." The animals "were so feeble and poor that they could scarce carry the little camp [equipment] which [Smith] had along." Traveling across the western deserts and over the Sierra Nevada, Smith and his companions had been forced to go for two days at a time without water and to eat their horses as the exhausted animals gave out.

In the years following Lewis and Clark's expedition, Rocky Mountain fur trappers accomplished important exploration in the West. Some crossed paths with British fur traders in the Oregon country and others drifted south to the Mexican towns of Taos and Santa Fe. Wherever they roamed, the American trappers left a lasting impression among the Native Americans, Mexicans, and British that the United States had established a presence in the West. And, as they crossed and recrossed mountain ranges, rivers, and prairies in search of furs and adventure, these rough, independent men found the most reliable routes across the country, which pioneer families would follow in the coming decades.

But the mountain man's era was short-lived. As early as 1833, the popularity of beaver hats was giving way to a new trend for silk hats. Fur prices plummeted. By 1840, with beaver populations dwindling from years of overtrapping, the once-prosperous trade ended. Many of the mountain men remained in the West, where they could continue to sleep in the open air and wander as they pleased. Some worked as scouts for the army, or guided wagon trains during the early years of the Oregon Trail. Others settled down to farm in Oregon's Willamette Valley or went to seek their fortune in California's gold fields. Whatever new life they chose, the mountain men brought their western characteristics with them—courage, self-reliance, humor, and ambition. ✿

3

Fort Vancouver

British Stronghold in the Pacific Northwest

As a young farm boy in New Hampshire, John Ball dreamed of traveling beyond the low hills near his family's home. His father expected all of the children to help tend the farm, and from an early age, John spent his days lugging water from the spring, driving the cows to and from the pasture, feeding the chickens, and raking the hay. When there was time, he explored the nearby woods, climbing trees and wading through streams. John loved to read, too, and knew the world was large and full of adventures. Sometimes, his father would tell him about their neighbor, John Ordway, who had traveled west as a member of Lewis and Clark's expedition, and John would imagine paddling a canoe in unknown lands, meeting Indians and hunting wild animals.

Eventually Ball went away to school and became a lawyer in New York, but he continued to dream about traveling west. Remembering Ordway's experience, he knew that it was possible for an ordinary man—like himself—to make the incredible trek.

In January 1832, having "worked hard all [his] life," the thirty-eight-year-old Ball decided to act on his dream. He wrote to Nathaniel Wyeth, an ambitious New England ice merchant who was planning to establish a fur-trading business on the Northwest Coast, and arranged to travel to Oregon with his party. That March, Ball met Wyeth's party in Baltimore. They went by railroad and steamboat to Missouri, where they joined a three-hundred-horse supply train that mountain man William Sublette was leading to the annual trappers' rendezvous. Leaving "civilization and all the comforts of social life behind," Wyeth's men began the long trip across the plains of Louisiana Territory.

Ball was surprised to find that he "stood this change of life . . . about as well as the mountaineers." Each day, he looked forward to the march by horseback and watched the changing landscape with interest. At night, he spread a buffalo robe on the ground, wrapped a blanket around his

In 1792, the American sea captain Robert Gray discovered the mouth of the Columbia River, opening the inland Northwest to European trade. The powerful river spews sand into the ocean, causing constantly shifting sandbars. The result is a treacherous, frothing surf that obscured it from other explorers such as Captains James Cook and George Vancouver.

On that eventful May morning, Chinook Indians paddled out to greet Gray's ship, the *Columbia Rediviva*. The Americans stayed for more than a week and traded copper, cloth, and nails for sea otter furs and beaver pelts. Their success encouraged trading ships to regularly cross the dangerous surf.

In the ongoing competition with Spain, Russia, and Great Britain for control of the Oregon country, the United States used Gray's discovery—as well as Lewis and Clark's expedition and John Jacob Astor's one-time settlement at Astoria—as claims to the land. By the mid-1820s, Spain had agreed to remain south of the forty-second parallel and Russia had pulled north of 54°40´, leaving just the United States and Great Britain to argue over Oregon. Until American pioneers began flooding into Oregon in the 1840s, the powerful Hudson's Bay Company effectively ruled the territory. But in 1846, the two countries negotiated a treaty that split Oregon at the forty-ninth parallel, causing the British to retreat northward.

feet, covered himself with a cloak, and slept soundly in the open air. While Ball enjoyed his new life, many of Wyeth's men became "disheartened and disgusted" with the hardships of wilderness travel. When the group reached the rendezvous, almost half of the men decided to turn east again with Sublette's pack train. Ball, Wyeth, and ten men continued west.

As they descended the Rocky Mountains, they left the boundary of the United States and entered the Oregon country. Since 1818, the United States and Great Britain had agreed to jointly occupy the remote region west of the mountains. Yet aside from sea traders along the coast, few Americans had ventured there. In addition to numerous Native American tribes, the area's main inhabitants were employees of the powerful British fur-trading company—the Hudson's Bay Company. Founded in 1670, the firm had developed immensely profitable operations in the Great Lakes and Hudson Bay regions of eastern Canada. In the early 1820s, the company expanded into the Pacific Northwest by merging with its strongest rival, the forty-year-old North West Company, and absorbing the smaller firm's western operations.

In the Oregon wilderness, Hudson's Bay men built small forts and stocked them with trade goods—metal tools, wool blankets, and strings of glass beads—which they exchanged with the Indians for beaver, fox, mink, bear, and otter furs. In addition, the company hired trappers to work in fur

Many Native American tribes called Hudson's Bay employees "cloth men." Their sturdy wool clothing, often topped by a warm Scottish cap, distinguished them from American mountain men, who were usually clad in buckskin pants and shirt. To keep American competitors out of Oregon, the Hudson's Bay Company overtrapped the Snake River Valley and surrounding lands. Company officials hoped this "fur desert" would discourage Rocky Mountain trappers from moving westward.

brigades. Groups of forty or more rugged men, often accompanied by their wives and children, would trap an assigned area for weeks or months at a time, returning with their pack horses piled high with pelts. Unlike the American mountain men, who exchanged their furs once a year at the rendezvous, Hudson's Bay employees turned in their furs at the numerous company forts that dotted the region's rivers and streams. From these inland posts, the furs were sent by canoe downstream toward the Pacific Ocean.

One hundred miles from the coast, at the confluence of the Willamette and Columbia Rivers, stood Fort Vancouver, the company's Northwest headquarters. Inside its high stockade walls, employees sorted pelts, sewed

The Chinook Jargon

More often than not, when fur traders met, one spoke a language the other could not understand. When this happened on the West Coast, traders relied on the Chinook jargon to communicate basic phrases and ideas. The makeshift language developed from the combining of French, English, Russian, and Native American vocabularies. Because the Chinook jargon contained only a few hundred words, it could not clearly express complicated matters such as treaties and religious teachings. However, this didn't stop people from trying, which sometimes created serious misunderstandings.

(The spelling of Chinook words varies widely; because it was primarily a spoken—not written—language, some words have been recorded in as many as fifteen different spellings.)

Sample Words

skookum	strong; powerful
eena	a beaver
Boston	an American
muckamuck	food; meal; to eat
tyee	a chief
chee	new
nowitka	yes; all right; certainly
canim	a canoe
kliminawhit	to lie
chuck	water
piah	fire
glease	grease
glease piah	a candle

Sample Phrases

Mika ticky mahsh okoke pish?	Will you sell that fish?
Kunsih chikamin ticky?	What is the price of it?
Olo na chuck miku?	Are you thirsty?
Mika ticky muckamuck?	Would you like something to eat?
Chako yukwa, sikhs.	Come here, friend.

them into water-tight bundles bound with elkskin, and shipped them to company headquarters in London. In return, supplies were sent to the fort on ships that sailed south from England, around Cape Horn at the tip of South America, and north to the Columbia River. Fort Vancouver also maintained connections with Hudson's Bay operations in eastern Canada. Following a complicated route of hazardous rivers, lakes, shallow streams, and waterfalls, "express" boats shuttled men, mail, and small shipments across the continent. This annual cycle of fur gathering, with the arrival and departure of inland boats and oceangoing ships, established a rhythm of life at the fort.

When Ball arrived at Fort Vancouver on October 29, 1832, he was surprised at the warm reception his rough and tumble party received from Dr. John McLoughlin, the fort's chief factor, or head agent. The six-foot-four-inch McLoughlin invited Ball to stay at the fort as a guest, but Ball insisted on earning his keep. So McLoughlin

Fort Vancouver
February 23, 1833

[Dear Parents:]
My health has been uniformly good ever since I saw you some fifteen months ago. . . . I wrote you from the mountains and hope my letters were received. . . .

Here I have been in comfortable quarters, teaching a few boys and enjoying the conveniences of home and good living. This is a post of the Hudson's Bay Company, which extends its trade of furs from Canada to this place. . . . I have been civilly treated by them, although I possessed no introductory letters or anything to recommend me. . . . Little can be brought under any circumstances across such an extent of wilderness. . . .

I have seen the country the description of which John Ordway gave you so interestingly when he returned from his tour with Lewis and Clark in 1806. The natives with their flattened heads are nearly the same. . . . They have changed their skin dress to a considerable extent for cloth. . . . Some have adopted the dress of the whites.

[Your loving son,]
John Ball

*"So I went . . . to look on the broad Pacific [Ocean], with nothing
between me and Japan. Standing . . . with the waves washing my feet,
was the happiest hour of my long journey. . . . I returned to camp
feeling I had not crossed the continent in vain."*

John Ball, November 9, 1832

asked him to set up a school to teach the children at the fort, including
the chief factor's son, David.

Ball found the outpost to be a bustling community. Six days a week,
employees rose at dawn and worked until dusk. Inside the fort, men
cleaned and packed furs, made sea biscuits and bread in the large bak-
ery ovens, wrote copies of company records and correspondence, and
tended the company store. Other employees plowed company fields,
chopped and milled timber, and tended livestock. Each man had a carefully assigned duty, and McLoughlin oversaw every detail. On Sundays,
church services were held. And when the men had free time, they competed in shooting contests and horse races, went swimming, or fished in
nearby streams and ponds.

McLoughlin kept a well-stocked library, too, adding new books and
papers from London each year. Even employees at distant inland posts
could request items and have them sent by the next canoe trip. Fort
Vancouver under Dr. McLoughlin's leadership seemed less a remote fur-
trade post than an energetic, frontier community. In 1836, a missionary
named Narcissa Whitman called Fort Vancouver the "New
York of the Pacific," so pleased was she with its
conveniences and comforts.

Nowhere else in Oregon could one find
such an array of goods and services. The
company store sold finished goods from
England—guns, pots and pans, bolts of
fine-spun cloth, paper, pens, needles, and
scissors—but most items were produced

*The Native Americans called John
McLoughlin the White-Headed Eagle because
his shoulder-length hair was prematurely gray.
As chief factor, McLoughlin was responsible
for the entire Columbia District operations—
everything from hiring employees and settling
trade disputes with Native Americans to overseeing
orders for the company store and checking the
detailed records of each season's fur harvest.*

at the fort itself. Skilled blacksmiths molded and hammered out nails, traps, and hinges, and repaired knives, hatchets, and other tools. Farmers grew corn, wheat, peas, oats, and potatoes. And orchards, started from plant cuttings carefully stored on the long ship voyage, yielded crops of plums, cherries, apples, and peaches. There was even fresh milk, butter, and cheese from a small herd of cattle McLoughlin had purchased in California.

The mix of employees added to the atmosphere: Irishmen, Scotsmen, and Englishmen from the British Isles; French-Canadians and Iroquois Indians from the Great Lakes area; Hawaiians (then referred to as Sandwich Islanders, Kanakas, or Owyhees); and a variety of Native Americans. Within the walls of the fort, and in the small village of houses that sprouted up outside, people spoke French, English, and Chinook

jargon—a combination of European and Native American vocabularies, as well as a smattering of other languages. Their clothing ranged from tailored coats and calico dresses to wool jackets and Indian moccasins.

After a winter of teaching, Ball was well-acquainted with Fort Vancouver life. However, he hadn't traveled across the continent with ambitions to work for a British fur company, so he decided to strike out and try his hand at farming. Again, he had to rely on the hospitality of McLoughlin as Fort Vancouver was the only supply point for hundreds of miles in any direction. McLoughlin loaned him farming tools, seed, and horses. With only occasional help from a friend he had made on the journey from Baltimore, Ball built a small house and tiny barn, fenced his plot of land, and broke a large field for planting.

He soon discovered that outside of the Hudson's Bay Company, an

Established in 1825, Fort Vancouver was the largest white settlement and a hub of activity for the entire Northwest. Under McLoughlin's leadership, the company produced so much food it was able to sell shipments to Russian fur traders in Alaska.

In 1810, McLoughlin married Marguerite Wadin McKay, the daughter of a Swiss trader and a Cree Indian woman. Like many fur-trade couples, they married "in the fashion of the country," or without an official religious ceremony. Unlike some white trappers and traders, McLoughlin treated his part-Indian wife with great love and respect. Many others treated their Native American wives poorly and left them if a better opportunity arose.

independent farmer had few people to rely on. Ball had trouble finding anyone to help him with his farming. He struggled to protect himself from thieves and suffered through "fever and ague." The sickness was probably related to a malaria epidemic that swept the area between 1829 and 1833. While few Europeans or Americans died of the disease, whole villages of Chinook and Kalapuyan Indians were wiped out. Since European and American seafarers began frequenting the Northwest Coast in the 1770s, local tribes had been decimated by diseases such as measles, smallpox, and influenza, to which they had no natural immunity. And when the British, and later the Americans, began to occupy their lands, the devastated Willamette and Columbia Valley Indians offered little resistance.

Ball soon recovered from the fever, but he was weary of his isolated life. In the fall of 1833, having decided that there was "no prospect of any settlers and no society," he abandoned his efforts. "Sick and discouraged," he bought passage aboard a trading ship and returned East after stops in San Francisco and the Sandwich Islands.

Little did John Ball realize that he was only a few years ahead of his time. The arrival of American missionaries in the mid-1830s added a new dimension to Columbia River life, and the 1840s proved an even greater turning point for Oregon. Inspired by reports of free land in a hospitable climate, groups of Americans began migrating west of the Rockies in larger and larger numbers. Some took the route to California, but thousands headed for Oregon country. Like Ball, the newly arrived Americans were interested in settling and farming the area. While they established themselves, they were glad to rely on the Hudson's Bay Company for supplies and medical assistance, but their goal was to be independent of the British.

With the American population increasing by leaps and bounds, tempers rose over who had rights to what lands. The United States and Great Britain realized their 1818 agreement to jointly occupy Oregon would no longer work. In 1846, the two nations signed a new treaty dividing Oregon at the forty-ninth parallel from the Rocky Mountains to the

Three years after the death of her husband in 1857, Marguerite (identified as Margaret on her tombstone) McLoughlin passed away and was buried by his side in Oregon City.

Pacific Ocean. This meant Fort Vancouver was officially on American soil. Having anticipated the treaty's terms, the Hudson's Bay Company had already begun to shift its Northwest headquarters north to Vancouver Island. The company had hoped to help claim more of Oregon for the British, but the incoming tide of American settlers and dwindling fur profits in southern Oregon convinced the British to move northward.

Dr. McLoughlin, who had devoted twenty years of his life to building Fort Vancouver into a prosperous community, fell from favor with company officials. McLoughlin had made a practice of aiding American immigrants and missionaries who arrived exhausted at the end of the Oregon Trail. He did it mostly out of goodwill but also, he argued, to increase company profits by selling them goods from the company store. Forced into early retirement in 1846, McLoughlin and his wife built a house on a favorite plot of land near the Willamette River. They lived the rest of their lives in Oregon City, an American town not far from where John Ball had tried to settle thirteen years earlier. Had the adventurous lawyer remained in Oregon, he might have spent his retirement next door to the man many came to call the "Father of Oregon." ✺

4

Place of the Rye Grass

The Whitman Mission

ON A COLD FEBRUARY DAY IN 1845, Narcissa Whitman took a break from her chores to write to her friend, Laura Brewer. "My Dear Mrs. Brewer," she began. "I have seated myself to write, although my baby is whining and the children are busy about me like so many bees." She went on to describe the past winter months—caring for her eleven adopted children at her home near the Walla Walla River—then addressed the letter to Wascopam, the small Methodist mission where Mrs. Brewer lived.

Narcissa and her husband Marcus worked as missionaries in the Oregon country. They believed that Native Americans lived a less advanced existence, and that teaching them Christianity would better their lives and save their souls.

These portraits of Narcissa and Marcus Whitman were created after their deaths from descriptions given by people who knew them.

"Tell mother I am a very good housekeeper on the prairie. I wish she could just take a peep at us while we are sitting at our meals. Our table is the ground, our table-cloth is an India-rubber cloth used when it rains as a cloak. . . . For my part I fix myself as gracefully as I can, sometimes on a blanket, sometimes on a box, just as it is convenient. Let me assure you of this, we relish our food none the less for sitting on the ground while eating."

Narcissa Whitman, in a letter to her brother and sister, June 3, 1836

For nine years, Marcus and Narcissa had lived among the Cayuse Indians at Waiilatpu, which meant Place of the Rye Grass. Their life was unlike what Narcissa had imagined it would be when, at the age of twenty-seven, she volunteered and was accepted for service with the American Board of Commissioners for Foreign Missions, an organization supported by the Congregational, Presbyterian, and Dutch Reformed Churches. On February 18, 1836, the devout and confident Narcissa married Marcus Whitman, a thirty-four-year-old doctor. The very next day, they set off on a twenty-five-hundred-mile journey to the wilds of the Oregon country. Narcissa and Eliza Spalding, the only other woman in the party, were the first white women to cross the western plains and the Rocky Mountains to the Pacific Northwest.

During her honeymoon trip, Narcissa learned to forgo the refined middle-class way of life to which she was accustomed. She and Marcus slept in a crowded tent; cooked and ate out of tin dishes; lived on a diet of buffalo meat for weeks on end (either freshly roasted or dried in tough, dirty strips); and gathered buffalo dung for fuel. Of this practice, she wrote to her family, "I suppose now [sister] Harriet will make up a face . . . but if she was here she would be glad to have her supper cooked at any rate in this scarce timber country."

As hard as it had been to leave her family and friends, Narcissa remained healthy and optimistic during the journey. Since the age of fifteen, she had felt a calling to serve God in this way. Each month, Narcissa read exciting stories in the board's newsletter, the *Missionary Herald*, about devoted women, scattered in exotic locations around the world—Cuba, India, Africa, and the Sandwich Islands. Narcissa envisioned herself making similar sacrifices among an appreciative group of natives, who would listen to her teachings and convert to Christianity. She imagined that the letters she wrote to her family would be published and would inspire other young women and men to volunteer for service. She firmly believed that she and her husband would earn eternal salvation through their endeavors to save the "benighted heathens."

Yet, when Narcissa arrived at Waiilatpu, the site near the Walla Walla River where Marcus had chosen to build their mission, she was homesick for her family and friends and uncomfortable among the Cayuses. The Indians' habit of entering her home unannounced made Narcissa feel as if she had no privacy. In addition, with her New England sensibilities, she thought the Cayuses were dirty and their habit of handling her furnishings left her home in disarray. She learned only a few simple words in the Nez Percé language, so the best she could do was to stutter halting phrases. Feeling self-conscious and awkward, Narcissa was unable to accept the customs and appearances of the people among whom she had chosen to live.

Nevertheless, she and Marcus worked hard to build the mission into a thriving farm, with a large garden and a field of corn, a sawmill,

Dr. John McLoughlin, the Hudson's Bay Company chief factor, greeted the Whitmans and Spaldings at Fort Vancouver near the end of their journey. Henry and Eliza Spalding went on to build a house and school among the Nez Percé Indians at Lapwai, 110 miles inland from the Whitmans' home on the Walla Walla River.

The Whitmans and Spaldings were not the first missionaries to arrive in Oregon. Two years earlier, a young Methodist minister named Jason Lee traveled west and, with the help of McLoughlin, settled in the Willamette Valley. Lee built a school and held services for the Chinook and other local tribes, but turned most of his energy to promoting American settlement of Oregon. He wrote numerous letters and traveled East to deliver speeches in which he described Oregon as a promised land for pioneer settlers.

"If you are thinking to become a missionary, you would do well to write a sermon on the word PATIENCE every day. . . . You will have more need of her by and by than ever you can have while you remain at home."

Narcissa Whitman, in a letter to her brother, March 12, 1842

a smokehouse, and a herd of cattle. Each week, some Indians would show up for their Sunday services and Bible study classes. A few prayed on a daily basis, but there were no real converts. Narcissa focused on raising her young daughter, Alice Clarissa, who was born during their first winter at Waiilatpu. But tragedy struck shortly after the little girl's second birthday. One day, while her mother was reading inside the house, Alice wandered outside. When Narcissa realized she hadn't heard her daughter's voice in some time, she rushed outside. The search

Through their work at the Waiilatpu mission, the Whitmans believed they were "saving the souls" of the Cayuse Indians by encouraging them to adopt Christianity and a settled American lifestyle. Much as the Cayuses had difficulty comprehending the history and meaning of Christianity, the Whitmans failed to understand that the Cayuses had a complex culture of their own, with deeply spiritual religious customs. Instead, the missionaries tried to forbid the Indians from practicing any traditional ceremonial dances or rituals.

confirmed her worst fears: Alice had fallen into the creek that flowed near the house and drowned.

The next few years were extremely difficult for Narcissa, who was devastated by the loss of her daughter. Marcus was traveling more, and Narcissa felt friendless and alone among the Indians.

Although she lacked the necessary patience and understanding to work closely with people who were so different from her, Narcissa discovered that she could be a very good—if extremely strict—mother. She and Marcus had not had any more children since Alice's death, but as it turned out, more children would come Narcissa's way than she had ever dreamed of.

First, Narcissa agreed to care for Mary Ann Bridger and Helen Mary Meek, the daughters of fur trappers James Bridger and Joseph Meek. (Bridger had been a friend of Marcus Whitman since 1835, when the doctor cut a three-inch iron arrowhead out of his back.) Both of the girls had Native American mothers.

One morning a year and a half later, Narcissa greeted two elderly Indian women at her door. They brought a "miserable-looking child, a boy between three and four years old," whom they wished to leave with Narcissa. The boy's

Explaining Christianity to the Indians was no easy task. The Whitmans and Spaldings struggled to find ways to explain their religion in the Noz Poroć language, which lacked words for Christian concepts. To bypass the language barrier, Henry Spalding designed a teaching tool called the Protestant Ladder. The six-foot-long chart depicted the story of Jesus Christ and his disciples in the middle column. The Ladder also showed pictures symbolic of the path to heaven and the road to hell.

"A tide of immigration appears to be moving this way rapidly. What a few years will bring forth we know not. . . . Instead of two lonely American females we now number fourteen, and soon [may be twenty or more]."

Narcissa, in a letter to her mother, May 2, 1840

father, a Spaniard, had abandoned his son to work in the mountains, and his mother had run off with another Indian. The boy was "dirty, covered with body and head lice, and starved." With little convincing, Narcissa agreed to take care of him, too. "[I] could not shut my heart against him," she wrote.

In 1843, Narcissa's family grew again when Marcus brought his thirteen-year-old nephew, Perrin Whitman, to live at the mission. And the next year, Narcissa temporarily took in "two English girls, Ann and Emma Hobson, one thirteen and the other seven," the motherless daughters of a wagon train emigrant. The girls "were so urgent" to stay with her that Narcissa could not refuse, though she "felt unwilling to increase [her] family." Later that year, with their house crowded and bustling, the Whitmans' charity would be tested even further.

Beginning in 1841, wagon trains had begun to straggle in each fall and the Whitman mission became a refuge for weary American emigrants. Exhausted and in need of supplies, the travelers stopped to rest before continuing on to the Willamette Valley. On October 9, 1844, Marcus wrote to his parents: "Our family had the important addition of an orphan family of seven children whose parents both died on the road to this country." The oldest boy was fourteen, the youngest child only five months old. One of the children, nine-year-old Catherine, had suffered a broken leg when she fell under one of the wagon wheels. Other members of their wagon train had cared for the children the best they could, but with winter approaching and new homes to build, none of the families could offer to take them in. Again the Whitmans came to the rescue.

Most of the children were old enough to help around the house and farm, and Narcissa found herself orchestrating three meals a day, prayers and school lessons, weekly clothes washings, and countless other chores. Her life buzzed with activity, and she was happier than she'd been in years with her newfound family. Her work among the Indians was largely forgotten, though Marcus continued to preach and to toil with them on the farm.

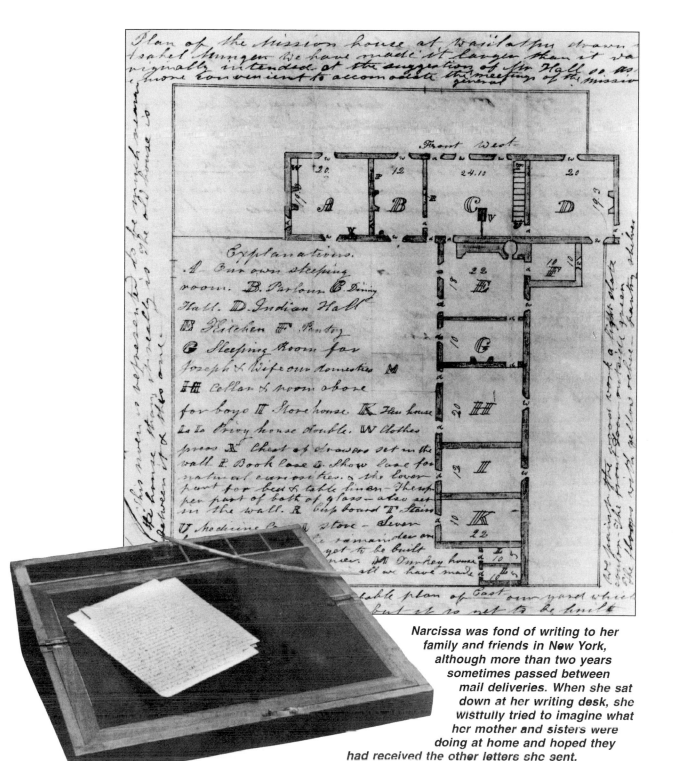

Narcissa was fond of writing to her family and friends in New York, although more than two years sometimes passed between mail deliveries. When she sat down at her writing desk, she wistfully tried to imagine what her mother and sisters were doing at home and hoped they had received the other letters she sent.

In this letter to her parents, written in May 1840, Narcissa included a plan of the new mission house. She labeled the rooms as follows: "A. Our own sleeping room. B. Parlor. C. Dining Hall. D. Indian Hall. E. Kitchen. F. Pantry. G. Sleeping room for Joseph and wife, our domestics. H. Cellar. I. Storehouse. K. Hen house. LL. Privy house—double."

"We are in the midst of excitement and prejudice on all sides, both from Indians and passing immigrants."

Narcissa Whitman, in a letter to her parents, October 1844

The Cayuse and Nez Percé Indians at first had welcomed the Whitmans and their fellow missionaries. They thought Christianity would give them the spiritual power and material wealth the white people seemed to control. But the Indians' hopes for newfound strength did not materialize. Marcus and Narcissa encouraged the Cayuses to completely change their lifestyle: to plant crops instead of fishing, hunting, and root gathering; to abandon their nomadic traditions and live in one place year-round; to speak English instead of Nez Percé; and to give up their native religion and adopt the prayers and customs of Christianity. In addition, the Indians were becoming increasingly angry at the annual arrival of wagon trains. They knew the emigrants wanted to settle on their land and felt that the Whitmans were betraying them by selling food and supplies to the travelers and encouraging them to stay.

A growing number of Cayuses became convinced that the missionaries were plotting against them. In March 1843, Marcus wrote to his brother, "[The Cayuses] have been led to believe that deceitful measures are being taken to rob them of their land, to kill them all off." While Whitman never purposefully tried to harm the Indians, it was true that he supported the settlement of their land by American emigrants. The doctor believed that if the Indians refused Christianity, they had no right to stand in the way of white settlers, whom he considered to be more civilized. The underlying assumption was that American settlers would put the land and natural resources to better use and were therefore more deserving.

In 1847, a measles epidemic broke out. The disease proved far more deadly to the Cayuses than to the Americans, and rumors spread that Dr. Whitman was poisoning the Indians. Other missionaries, Hudson's Bay employees, and friendly Indians warned the Whitmans that their lives were in danger, but Marcus and Narcissa were distracted caring for the sick. After eleven years at Waiilatpu, during which they'd survived many past scares with angry tribal members, they felt fairly sure that the fiery accusations would die down, and they delayed making a decision to leave the mission until spring.

On November 29, a dark, autumn day, Narcissa went in to her kitchen to get some milk for the sick children. She was surprised to find the room crowded with angry Indians. As she left, Marcus entered to take

The tomahawk believed to be the one that killed Marcus Whitman

care of a man named Tomahas, who was asking for medicine. From the other room, Narcissa heard voices rising, then the *crack!* of a gun. Chaos erupted, as a group of Cayuse men attacked the mission residents. In the kitchen, Marcus was hit twice with a tomahawk and slashed in the face. Narcissa tried to calm the children in the house, but a bullet came through the window and struck her. By morning, the Whitmans and eleven others were dead, and forty-seven men, women, and children had been taken hostage.

One month later, the chief agent of the Hudson's Bay Company, who lived downriver at Fort Vancouver, talked the Cayuses into exchanging the captives for a ransom, which included blankets, shirts, guns, tobacco, and ammunition from the company's stores.

Narcissa had often referred to her vocation as a "sacrifice," and in the end, it proved to be just that. She and Marcus had failed in their goal of converting the Cayuse Indians to Christianity, but their work led to other accomplishments. In 1843, while returning from a trip east, Marcus had helped lead the first large wagon train on the Oregon Trail. Until their deaths in 1847, he and Narcissa aided hundreds of pioneers who used their mission as a rest stop on the trail. Along with other missionaries who inhabited Oregon, the Whitmans helped prove to American families that a decent lifestyle could be attained in the Far West—that wagons could be taken across the Rocky Mountains, that women and children could live in the Oregon "wilderness," and that emigration was an opportunity worth considering. ❂

5

Defending Their Homeland

The Black Hawk War

BLACK HAWK, LEADER OF THE SAUK and Fox Indian nation, and a band of twenty warriors rode through the hills toward Saukenuk, their summer home. The village of one hundred bark-covered lodges was built on a point of land between the Rock and Mississippi Rivers in present-day Illinois. It was an ideal site. The rivers teemed with fish; the nearby woods were filled with deer, elk, raccoons, and rabbits; and the soil was fertile, allowing the Sauks and their allies, the Foxes, to grow fine crops of corn, pumpkins, squash, and beans. Black Hawk's warriors had been away for a year, fighting on the side of the British in the War of 1812. As they neared the village, Black Hawk spied a column of smoke rising from a hollow in the bluffs. Directing his party to continue home, he turned to investigate.

When he reached the small fire, Black Hawk recognized the old man crouched beside it. Black Hawk lit his pipe and offered it to his friend, who

Black Hawk's name in the Sauk language was Ma-ka-tai-me-she-kia-kiak. He took the name as a boy, after having a vision in which a Black Sparrow Hawk appeared as his personal protector.

"Why did the Great Spirit ever send the whites to this island [North America] to drive us from our homes and introduce among us poisonous liquors, disease, and death? *They should have remained on the Island where the Great Spirit first placed them."*

Black Hawk, from his autobiography, 1834

appeared to have been fasting for a long time. Black Hawk asked him what was wrong. In a feeble voice, the man told his tale.

Shortly after Black Hawk had left Saukenuk the previous fall, the old man and a small group had traveled down the Mississippi to camp for the winter, having been invited by a white family to come and hunt near them. The site was close to a U.S. Army fort, which the old man took care to visit, "to tell the white people that [he] and [his] little band were friendly, and that [they] wished to hunt in the vicinity." The commanding officer told him that they could hunt on the west side of the Mississippi and that "no person would trouble [them]." The band of Indians crossed the river, "pleased with this assurance of safety." Finding plenty of game, they settled in for the winter.

One day about two months later, the man's son went out to hunt. When he didn't return, the boy's mother fearfully alerted the others. A search party easily followed the boy's tracks in the snow and found the deer he had shot, skinned, and hung from a tree branch. There they also found the tracks of white men, leading across the river toward the fort. Tracing the path, the Indians discovered the boy lying dead. "His face was shot to pieces—his body stabbed in several places—and his head *scalped!*" Worst of all, the attackers had tied the young hunter's arms behind his back, leaving him completely defenseless against his killers.

The old man paused a long time and went on to tell Black Hawk that the boy's mother, his wife, had died soon after, too. Black Hawk took the man's hand and pledged to avenge the death of his son. Later that night, while Black Hawk was kindling the fire, his old friend died. In the morning, a party of Indians from the village helped the chief bury the man at the top of the bluff.

All along the wide, muddy-colored waters of the Mississippi River, similar acts of violence between white settlers and Indians had become commonplace. The strong-flowing river acted as a dividing line between the settled East and the western wilderness. At first, only a few mountain men, explorers, and missionaries ventured across. But as more families moved west to break frontier land for farming, they forced the Native American tribes who lived east of the river to move to the other side.

The expansion-minded leaders of the United States usually tried to satisfy the land-hungry settlers. Federal authorities negotiated treaties with Indian tribes, promising money and annual payment of goods for their lands. Sometimes, they used dishonest means to convince the Indians to sign the papers.

In 1804, the Sauk and Fox Indians signed a treaty with the United States. The agreement occurred when five Sauk chiefs traveled to St. Louis to settle a dispute over the murder of three white people at a small settlement on the Cuivre River, bringing with them the Sauk Indian accused of the crime. They hoped to win the man's pardon by offering presents to the victims' families—a common practice among Indians referred to as "wiping away the tears." When the Sauk chiefs met with William Henry Harrison, the governor of Indiana Territory who was hearing the case, Harrison said he would release the prisoner only if the Sauks would

*The powerful **Mississippi River** runs southward from the region west of Lake Superior to the Gulf of Mexico. European and American traders as well as U.S. Indian agents used the river to conduct business with Indian tribes along its route.*

"This is all myself or nation knew of the treaty of 1804. It has been explained to me since. I find, by that treaty, all our country, east of the Mississippi . . . was ceded to the United States for $1,000 a year! I will leave it to the people of the United States to say whether our nation was properly represented in this treaty? Or whether we received a fair compensation for the extent of country ceded by those four individuals? I could say much about this treaty, but I will not, at this time. It has been the origin of all our difficulties."

Black Hawk, from his autobiography, 1834

give up some of their lands in return. The chiefs had no authority to strike such a deal without the permission of other tribal members, but after being showered with gifts and served countless drinks of alcohol, they signed their names to the agreement.

The five chiefs didn't realize the meaning of the document. Like most Native American tribes, the Sauks believed that land was a gift from the Great Spirit to be used by all living things. A tribe could control an area of land and defend it from other hunters, but no one could "own" a piece of the universal earth. In the treaty, the Sauks thought they had given the Americans the right to use the land, but not given the land itself so that no one else could set foot on it.

From this point forward, the relationship between the Sauk and Fox nation and the Americans would be troubled. The mistrust had deepened with the outbreak of the War of 1812. When the United States and Great Britain came to blows, the Sauk Indians were caught in the middle. Their lands lay between Indiana and Louisiana Territories in the United States, near British landholdings in Canada. One of the reasons the two countries had gone to war was that the United States believed Great Britain was stirring up Indians on the frontier, spurring them to violence against American settlers as a means of halting their westward advance.

In the summer of 1812, U.S. President James Madison invited several Sauk leaders to Washington, D.C., where he asked them to remain neutral in the war despite their long-standing alliances with British traders. The president also told them that the British, whom the Sauk Indians depended on for supplies, would no longer be allowed to travel on the Mississippi or trade with the Sauks. He promised that the Indians "would be well supplied by an American trader" instead. The Sauk chiefs impressed upon him that "the British traders always gave [them] credits in the fall, for guns, powder, and goods." This enabled them "to hunt, and clothe [their] families" during the winter, before paying the traders back with deer, muskrat, and beaver skins the following spring. Without receiving goods on credit each fall, the Sauks said, their families would not make it through the winter. President Madison replied that the American trader at Fort Madison "would have plenty of goods . . . and would supply [them] on credit, as the British traders had done."

The next fall, after harvesting their crops, the Sauk and Fox families went to Fort Madison to meet the American trader. "He said he was happy to hear that we intended to remain at peace," Black Hawk recalled. The American had "a large quantity of goods . . . but remarked that *he had received no instructions to furnish us anything on credit!—nor could he give us any without receiving the pay for them on the spot!*"

With no other means of obtaining goods for the snowy winter season, the Sauks turned back to Saukenuk. There they found a British trader waiting for them with two full boatloads of goods—offered on credit. The Sauks listened with open ears when the trader invited them to join British forces gathered at Green Bay to fight against the

In August 1825, William Clark, U.S. Superintendent of Indian Affairs, and Governor Lewis Cass of Michigan Territory met with leaders of the Santee Sioux, Ojibwa, Winnebago, Potawatomi, Iowa, and Sauk and Fox tribes in Prairie du Chien, Wisconsin. The result was the drawing of formal borders between tribal lands, which helped curb intertribal warfare in the Upper Mississippi region. The defined boundaries also made it easier for the government to negotiate for Indian land in the following years, hastening relocation of the tribes.

During the 1700s, the Fox tribe had confederated with the Sauk Indians, seeking their protection from hostile French traders. By late in that century, political leaders recognized the tribes as one nation and negotiated with them as such.

Americans. After the insulting trading fiasco at Fort Madison, Black Hawk declared, "Here ended all hopes of our remaining at peace—having been *forced into* WAR *by being* DECEIVED!"

For three years, Black Hawk and his warriors and other Indian tribes fought alongside the British, hoping to defeat the Americans. In 1815, Great Britain and the United States reached a truce with the Treaty of Ghent. But the Sauks, despite having fought well, had settled none of their grievances. To make matters more confusing, in 1816 Black Hawk signed a new treaty with the Americans, which he understood to be a peace treaty acknowledging the end of the war. Later he discovered that by signing it he was confirming the despised 1804 Treaty. "Here, for the

"As the settlements progressed towards us, we became worse off and more unhappy. Many of our people . . . would go near to the settlements to hunt—and, instead of saving their skins to pay the trader for goods furnished them in the fall, would sell them to the settlers for whiskey! and return in the spring with their families, almost naked, and without the means of getting anything for them."

Black Hawk, from his autobiography, 1834

first time," he recalled, "I touched goose quill to the treaty—not knowing . . . that, by that act, I consented to give away my village. Had that been explained to me, I . . . never would have signed their treaty."

After the war, Black Hawk found much had changed at Saukenuk. More American settlers had moved in, fencing off portions of the Sauks' hunting grounds to use for pastures and farmland. Some stole the Indians' corn, claiming the crops as their own, and burned the Indians' bark-covered houses. And in Black Hawk's absence, a young brave named Keokuk had encouraged the Sauks and Foxes to surrender their lands to the Americans and move west of the Mississippi. The tribe split into two groups, with one side listening to Black Hawk and the other to Keokuk.

Fifteen hundred Indians followed Keokuk to a new village on the Iowa River—west of the Mississippi. But for the next fifteen years, Black Hawk's group continued to live according to the tribe's long-standing traditions. During the winter, they hunted from temporary camps, wherever they could find the most game, and in the spring, they returned to their permanent lodges at Saukenuk to plant crops, fish in the river, and gather fruit and nuts from the woods. Black Hawk could not imagine doing anything else. "It was here that I was born," he explained, "and here lie the bones of many friends and relations. For this spot I [feel] a sacred reverence and never could consent to leave it, without being forced."

Finally, in June 1831, William Clark, the U.S. Superintendent of Indian Affairs (who had gained fame for his earlier explorations with Meriwether Lewis), sent federal troops to Rock River to force the Indians to leave. General Edmund P. Gaines met with Black Hawk. Gaines still hoped he could convince the Sauks to leave their home peacefully, partly because he was afraid he didn't have enough troops to win a fight if the Sauks joined forces with other Indian tribes. The general explained to the Indians, "The president (Andrew Jackson) is very sorry to be put to the trouble and expense of sending a large body of soldiers here, to remove you from the lands you have long since ceded to the United States."

Andrew Jackson, who became president in 1828, strongly supported the opening of Native American lands to white settlers. In May 1830, he convinced Congress to pass the Indian Removal Bill, which allowed for the relocation of tribes by force.

Black Hawk was infuriated. Although Keokuk and his followers had agreed to honor the terms of the 1804 and 1816 treaties, Black Hawk's group had never conceded to the sale of their lands. "*We* had never sold our country," he insisted. "And *we* are determined to hold on to our village!" After a few more angry words, the meeting ended and Gaines called for more troops.

Twenty days later, fourteen hundred members of the Illinois militia arrived. Unlike the federal soldiers under Gaines's command, the men in the militia were angry local settlers, ready to attack any Indian who crossed their path. Before Gaines could slow them down, they stormed into Saukenuk—but the town was empty! Black Hawk and his people, alerted by scouts, had slipped across the Mississippi during the night.

On June 30, Black Hawk and several warriors reappeared. Realizing they were outnumbered, they met General Gaines and, at last, agreed to leave Saukenuk. In return, Gaines promised Black Hawk's people that the local settlers would give them a year's supply of corn to make up for the unharvested crops the Sauks were abandoning. But as soon as Gaines left, the hostile militia chased away Black Hawk's people with gunfire, giving them only a small portion of the promised corn. Furious at the Americans for again breaking their word, Black Hawk vowed to reclaim his village. Over the next year, he enlisted the support of the Potawatomi, Chippewa, Kickapoo, and Winnebago Indians. He also received word that the British would send guns and ammunition from Canada.

In the spring of 1832, Black Hawk led two thousand men, women, and children across the river and headed north to Saukenuk. He planned to peacefully enter the village and plant new crops of corn. As they drew closer, Black Hawk learned that several hundred U.S. troops were stationed there, so he veered northeast to a friendly Winnebago village. The Potawatomis and several other tribes decided not to join him after all, and the British failed to support them with any supplies.

But it was too late for Black Hawk to turn back. An army battalion of more than 250 men was in pursuit of the Indians. When he received news of the troops, Black Hawk was temporarily separated from his people, and because he had only fifty warriors with him, he decided to

On May 20, 1832, a party of Potawatomi Indians massacred fifteen white settlers at the home of William Davis. The Potawatomis were avenging an earlier incident in which Davis severely whipped one of the Indians after they complained that a dam he built was interfering with their fishing. The only survivors of the massacre were Rachel and Sylvia Hall, who were swooped up and carried away by three Sauk Indians who were traveling with the Potawatomis. The girls were released unharmed eleven days later.

In his autobiography, Black Hawk earnestly stated, "I never did, nor have I any knowledge that any of my nation ever killed a white woman or child." Despite the warrior's peaceful intentions, the Black Hawk War resulted in the deaths of more than sixty settlers and soldiers, and as many as five hundred Indians from various area tribes.

surrender. He sent three warriors with a white flag in the direction of the battalion and another five men to follow and watch from a distance. As the first three Indians reached the troops, some soldiers spied the second party and shots rang out, killing one of the flag bearers. Jumping on their horses, the soldiers stormed onto the prairie expecting a large-scale Indian attack. Black Hawk and his warriors rushed to meet them, yelling and firing their guns. Some soldiers became confused and stampeded back to camp shouting that a thousand Indians were attacking. Soon the whole unit retreated. Black Hawk had won the "battle"!

When word of his success spread, bands of Potawatomis, Winnebagos, and Kickapoos launched their own small attacks, killing mostly white settlers—not soldiers—and blanketing the countryside with fear.

President Andrew Jackson learned of the settlers' terror and dispatched more troops to Illinois.

Black Hawk and his warriors fled with their families up the Rock River, hoping to escape to the other side of the Mississippi. Constantly changing their route to avoid the army, they were kept on the run for two and a half months. They hid in swamps and marshes, where they were plagued by mosquitoes. When their supplies ran out, they ate roots and bark to stay alive. Many older people died, and the children struggled

American settlers greatly feared Indian attacks. Stories of brutal murders, scalpings, and kidnapings circulated through frontier settlements, growing more fantastic with each telling. Sometimes they made it into print—such as the narrative War and Pestilence! *pictured to the right. (The young Hall women mentioned here were not related to Rachel and Sylvia, pictured on the preceding page.) Publishers failed to note that the frontier clashes proved just as frightening for the Native American families.*

to keep up. Growing weaker, they abandoned possessions they could no longer carry.

Finally, on August 1, they looped back to the Mississippi at the mouth of the Bad Axe River. While they feverishly worked to build canoes and rafts to cross the river, a steamboat approached. Black Hawk recognized the *Warrior*, so he raised a white flag and sent a brave to indicate that his sick, exhausted people were ready to surrender. The message was misinterpreted, and troops aboard the *Warrior* opened fire, instantly killing some Indians near the river's edge, before they could scramble to safety. After a two-hour battle, the *Warrior* steamed away to refuel. Black Hawk's people hid in the trees, and the chief left them to try to find help from a nearby Chippewa tribe. Two days later, before Black Hawk returned, a thirteen-hundred-man regiment caught the Indians trying to cross the river. As the chief later described, "they tried to give themselves up [but] the whites paid no attention . . . [and] commenced slaughtering them!" The warriors fought back with rifles and war clubs, while many of the women put children on their backs and started swimming across the river. Some drowned in the current, and sharpshooters took careful aim at others. In the midst of the chaos, the *Warrior* returned and joined in the firing.

Other Native American tribes already occupied the lands west of the Mississippi where the United States was encouraging the Sauks and Foxes to settle. When Black Hawk's people tested new hunting grounds to the north and west, they invited the hostilities of fierce warriors from tribes such as the Sioux.

Following the Black Hawk War, U.S. officials recognized Keokuk, who had stripped Black Hawk of his power, as the primary leader of the Sauks and Foxes. In 1847, a year before he died of dysentery, Keokuk posed for this photograph by Thomas Easterly.

Eight hours later, the Battle of Bad Axe was over. One hundred and fifty Indians were dead and thirty-nine had been taken prisoner. Days later, sixty-eight of the Indians who survived the Mississippi crossing were killed and scalped by hostile Sioux Indians on the other side. Black Hawk soon turned himself in and was taken to Jefferson Barracks, a military post near St. Louis.

A year later, the defeated chief returned to his nation at their new home in Iowa Territory. He settled in a small house on the Des Moines River with his wife, Singing Bird, and their sons and daughter. The family planted a garden and continued to hunt, struggling to follow their old ways. Black Hawk died in 1839 at the age of seventy-one.

Under pressure from government officials, Keokuk continued to sell Sauk and Fox lands to the United States. By 1842, to escape the frontier settlements, the tribe gave up its Iowa lands entirely and moved west of the Missouri River, to share lands with the Ottawa, Chippewa, and Kansas tribes. They had only meager success trying to farm the prairie ground and many difficulties finding enough animals to hunt.

The defeat of Black Hawk and the Sauk and Fox nation sent a message to other tribes that armed resistance to the United States was unlikely to succeed—although, with their lives and traditions as well as their lands at stake, many tribes continued the struggle. In the South, too, the United States forced once-powerful tribes such as the Creeks, Choctaws, Cherokees, and Chickasaws to move west. White cotton farmers and miners eagerly occupied their lands. By the 1840s, the United States had acquired more than 440 million acres from Native Americans. The government, in turn, sold much of the land to white settlers for as little as $1.25 an acre.

While frontier families planted crops on their new farmlands with hopes of a better life, the relocated Indians struggled to build homes on the unfamiliar plains west of the Mississippi. The harsh prairie climate made it difficult to raise crops, and the tribes competed for game on increasingly crowded hunting grounds. In addition, cholera and smallpox epidemics swept through their villages, killing thousands. For decades to come, the Americans' thirst for land continued to haunt the tribes. ✪

6

Westward, Ho!

Breaking the Oregon Trail

"April 21, 1847—Commenced our journey from La Porte, Indiana, to Oregon; made fourteen miles.

April 22—Made twelve miles; rain all day.

April 23—Made nineteen miles; traveled until dark. Ate a cold bite and went to bed chilly and cold, which is very disagreeable with a parcel of little children.

April 24—Made twelve miles.

April 25—Last night our cattle ran off, consequently we only made eleven miles."

WITH THIS HUMBLE START, thirty-nine-year-old Elizabeth Dixon Smith, her husband, Cornelius, and eight children, set off on a rigorous seven-month journey to Oregon, leaving behind forever their home and friends in Indiana. The family's lumber mill had burned, and rather than rebuild, the Smiths decided to head west. Elizabeth's neighbors, Paulina Foster and Cynthia Ames, made her promise to write from Oregon with all the details of the trip. The two Indiana women were curious—and worried—about how the Smith family would survive the long journey.

For generations, Americans had migrated westward—to Kentucky and Tennessee, then Indiana and Illinois, and across the Mississippi to Iowa and Missouri. Many were farmers who measured wealth in terms of landholdings. As the country's population continued to grow, pioneers pushed the American frontier westward, claiming Native American lands for their own as they went.

By 1847, travel on the Oregon Trail was a new, exciting, and risky prospect. Although there was little reliable information about the faraway territory, glowing newspaper editorials and published accounts of missionaries, fur traders, and government explorers convinced many that on the other side of the continent lay a healthy climate, with fertile farmland and good commercial prospects. It was all they needed to start a new life. Some traveled west to escape bad debts, a failed marriage, or a prison sentence, but most were like the Smiths, families looking for better opportunities. Soon, the two-thousand-mile route across rivers, plains, deserts, and mountains became a well-traveled path. The year Elizabeth Dixon Smith set out, about four thousand emigrants took to the Oregon Trail.

In late spring, groups of pioneers would gather near the start of the trail—in the frontier towns of Independence, Westport, and St. Joseph, on the banks of the Missouri River. Elizabeth's family arrived in St. Joseph on June 3. The town bustled with people, wagons, oxen, and horses. Blacksmiths, carpenters, and shop owners did a steady business outfitting

The first large group of emigrants to travel the Oregon Trail left Independence, Missouri, in the spring of 1843. Dr. Marcus Whitman accompanied the train of nine hundred people after a brief visit East to plea for continued support for his mission on the Walla Walla River. Whitman's frontier experience and medical knowledge proved invaluable, but his greatest advice was to keep moving forward, avoiding any delay, to ensure they crossed the Blue Mountains before the winter snows set in.

"In the late summer of 1848, Father returned from town and said: 'I have sold the farm and we will go to Oregon.' That was a great sorrow to me then as I dearly loved our home. From that time until March 1849 [my parents] were preparing for that six months' journey, through the wilderness inhabited by Indians."

Virginia Watson Applegate, recalling leaving her home near Springfield, Illinois, at the age of nine

travelers. This was the last chance to buy goods until Fort Laramie, a trading post 650 miles away on the North Platte River, where the selection would be scant and prices high. The Smiths bought a few additional supplies—"flour, cheese and crackers, and medicine."

Preparing to travel more than two thousand miles in a covered wagon was an immense undertaking. People agonized over which belongings to take and which to leave behind. Their four-by-ten-foot wagons had to hold bedding, extra clothing, dishes, utensils, gunpowder, lead for making bullets, tools, and furniture. Items such as books, dolls, mirrors, rocking chairs, silverware, and fine linens posed serious dilemmas. Many people tried to cram in every beloved item, whether or not it served a useful purpose, only to regret it later when their oxen wore out from the overly heavy load.

Food was an important consideration, too. Along the way, the emigrants hoped to hunt deer, antelope, buffalo, and wild birds, to pick berries and catch catfish and trout, but they couldn't rely on finding enough of any of these to survive the six- to seven-month journey. In the guidebooks that had recently begun to appear,

The pioneers built their wagons with well-seasoned hardwood such as maple, hickory, or oak. The wagons had to be light enough for the oxen to pull but sturdy enough to carry several thousand pounds of goods over uneven ground, withstanding violent hailstorms, scorching desert temperatures, and early winter snows. Some emigrants modified the farm wagons they already owned, while others had vehicles specially built for the trip.

Emigrants filled every last nook and cranny of their wagons. Among other things, they packed a long saw, a grab hoe, an ax, a plow, a toolbox, an iron chain, an extra rope, a frying pan, a kettle, a tin coffeepot, a butter churn, a candle mold, a candlestick, trunks, comforters, a medicine box, and lanterns.

One of the most-used items on the trail was the Dutch oven. The sturdy pot could be used to cook beans, bake bread, or stew fresh meat. Campfire cooks used the lip around the edge of the lid to pile coals on top, which hastened the cooking time.

people who had already made the trip recommended packing several hundred pounds of food per person:

- 200 pounds flour
- 75 pounds bacon
- 30 pounds pilot bread
- 5 pounds coffee
- 2 pounds tea
- 25 pounds sugar
- 1/2 bushel dried beans
- 1 bushel dried fruit
- 2 pounds saleratus (baking soda)
- 10 pounds salt
- 1/2 bushel cornmeal
- 1/4 bushel parched or ground corn
- 1 keg vinegar

Health was also a concern. Most wagons had a medicine chest packed with a hodgepodge of homemade and store-bought remedies. The travelers were sure to encounter illnesses and accidents—food poisoning, toothaches, snake bites, and broken bones—with no hope of seeing a doctor. Elizabeth felt, "Each family should have a box of physicking pills, a quart of castor oil, a quart of the best rum, and a large vial of peppermint essence."

The day after they left St. Joseph, the Smiths crossed the Missouri River to "Indian territory." With twenty-two wagons in their company, they had to double up the teams of oxen to haul the vehicles up a steep hill. The adventure had begun!

Turning west from the Missouri to the Platte River, the wagons' large, spoked wheels bounced and jostled over grassy prairie soil, their white canvas tops glistening in the sun. The oxen had plenty of freshly sprouted

Wagon train pioneers soon discovered they wouldn't need to churn butter until after they arrived in Oregon. Along the trail, they could make it simply by putting their milk in a pail. By the end of the day, the jostling of the wagon would produce several nice nuggets of butter.

From the rear axle of every covered wagon dangled a small, sticky tar bucket, used to lubricate the axles. The pioneers kept it filled with tar, oil, or cooking lard—or, in a pinch, with wolf or buffalo grease.

Not everyone who set out on the Oregon Trail was young and eager to start a new life. In 1846, at the age of sixty-six, widow Tabitha Brown traveled to Oregon with her eldest son's family. Her brother-in-law, retired sea captain John Brown, also accompanied the family—at the age of seventy-seven.

grass to munch during "nooning" (the mid-day rest) and at night. Most pioneers were excited to have finally started their journey, but some complained about the long days on the trail, fretting about the comfortable homes they had left behind.

Each evening, the travelers pulled the wagons into a circle and strung a chain connecting them. The oxen, milk cows, and saddle horses grazed for a few hours before they were herded inside the circle for the night to protect them from being stolen or wandering off. While cooking some bread and a pot of beans or stewed apples, the members of the train visited by their campfires and discussed their progress. After the concentrated effort to keep the wagons and livestock moving during the day, they enjoyed an hour or two of relaxation. In the Smiths' train, each night they had "plenty of music, with the flute and violin, and some dancing."

As the stars filled the broad night sky, the families turned in. Some slept in tents or in narrow beds inside their wagons. Others spread out on ground cloths in the open air. Following an agreed-upon schedule, the men took turns standing guard duty through the

Even on the open prairie, hundreds of miles from the nearest kitchen, pioneer women managed to mix and roll dough, filling it with a sweet mixture of dried fruit and sugar, to make apple pies.

"We have a cooking stove made of sheet iron, a portable table, tin plates and cups, cheap knives and forks (best ones packed away), camp stools, etc. We sleep in our wagons on feather beds. . . . We live on bacon, ham, rice, dried fruits, molasses, packed butter, bread, coffee, tea, and milk, as we have our own cows."

Sallie Hester, age fourteen, in camp near the Blue River (215 miles from St. Joseph), May 21, 1849

night. Waking before dawn to a quick bite of bread and bacon, they repacked their dishes, food, and bedding, unhooked the wagons, and hitched the oxen. Before the sun cleared the horizon, the westward journey through the dew-covered grass continued.

The families took turns leading the line of wagons. By mid-morning, the wagons in the rear suffered clouds of dust raised by those in front. In addition to the dust, the emigrants had to drink water from whatever streams, rivers, lakes, and ponds they passed. One pioneer, forced to drink water from a stagnant slough, woefully admitted, "We are obliged to use it, for it's all we have." Some people used a piece of cloth to siphon dirt from murky water; others scooped up the water and let it sit for a while, hoping the dirt would settle to the bottom. To hide the terrible flavor, many mixed in flavored vinegar or essence of lemon. The emigrants didn't realize that some contaminated water carried disease-spreading organisms, which caused people to sicken or die from cholera, typhoid fever, or diphtheria.

Less than a month after leaving St. Joseph, the Smiths' company encountered their first problems on the trail. On June 29, they awoke to find some of their oxen missing. "Here we were thousands of miles from any inhabitants and thus deprived of teams—an appalling situation," Elizabeth wrote. "We hunted every direction without success." The next day, the men searched as far as thirty miles from the camp, staying away all night looking for the animals.

Company morale dropped even lower when a group who had been hunting for food returned with one of their men dead. The pioneer had shot himself accidentally. "He left a wife and six small children," Elizabeth recorded. "The distress of his wife I cannot describe. He was an excellent man and very much missed." Despite the tragedy and the missing oxen, the company had to continue. "Had to take raw cattle, cows, or anything we could get," she described. "Some had to apply to other wagon trains for help; at last we moved off."

A Pioneer Train Constitution – 1849

We the undersigned, being desirous of forming ourselves into a company for the purpose of emigrating to the Sacramento Valley in California and believing that order, good conduct, and mutual support will more effectually enable us to . . . reach our destination, we hereby bind ourselves . . . to submit to all the rules and regulations herein.

We agree:

- That every wagon must have been approved by the Inspector appointed and must also be provided with a team, provision, arms, and ammunition.

- This Company shall be known by the name of the Sacramento Company and shall consist of not exceeding fifty teams.

- There shall be a Colonel and Adjutant who shall be elected by the Company, . . . and there shall be five Captains.

- Each of the above officers [may] be removed at any time by a majority of their electors.

- It shall be the duty of the Colonel to have full command as a military officer . . . to superintend all for the good order of said Company.

- The Adjutant shall act as secretary [and] keep a roll of every man's name in said Company.

- The duty of the Captains will be to take command of the guard each night in rotation.

- Every man attached to the Company except foresaid officers must keep guard or perform other duties according to his regular turn on the roll. . . . And if any be sick, his or their names must be supplied by the next name or names in order on the roll.

- The officers of the Company shall compose a court for the trial of offenses and . . . punishments awarded according to the offense committed.

- Drunkenness, sleeping on guard, and neglect of orders received from the Officers to be considered grievous offenses subjecting persons convicted . . . to expulsion.

- All quarreling and fighting shall be considered a violation of the rules and regulations of the Company.

- In case of any wagon being disabled and not being able to be repaired or any team being disabled . . . , the board of officers shall make such distribution of the load of said wagon among the other wagons.

- In case of the death of any member of the Company, an inventory of his effects shall be taken [and] said effects [distributed] to the friends or heirs.

Pioneers migrated west in wagon trains because they felt safer traveling as part of a group. Often the trains were made up of relatives, neighbors, or church members who hailed from the same town or county. During their first weeks on the trail, they elected leaders and wrote rules of conduct, which they called a constitution. The emigrants tried to anticipate problems—wagons breaking down, men falling asleep on guard duty, or quarrels getting out of hand. Even if they started out as friends, after four or five grueling months on the trail, many pioneers became irritated with fellow travelers.

*"At present there is one hundred and forty persons in our company.
We see thousands of buffalo and have to use their dung for fuel.
A man will gather a bushel in a minute; three bushels makes a
good fire. We call the stuff 'buffalo chips.'"*

Elizabeth Dixon Smith, June 23, 1847

Still following the Platte River, they branched off along the north fork, and the sight of a famous landmark soon cheered them. Visible for miles on the level plain, Chimney Rock towered more than five hundred feet in the air. "It is a curiosity indeed," Elizabeth wrote. She set off on foot with another woman to take a closer look at the strange rock formation. Before reaching the sandy-colored shaft, they encountered another unique feature of the Platte River Valley—its violent summer storms. "We had the most dreadful hailstorm that I ever witnessed," Elizabeth recalled after the ordeal. "Fortunately, we reached one of the foremost wagons just as the hail began to pelt us. It tore some of their wagon covers off, broke some [wagon] bows, and made horses and oxen run away. . . ." Often, the wind and hail severely bruised people and tore holes in their wagon tops.

The trail crossed rivers and streams that called for careful judgment. If the water was too deep, the pioneers floated their wagons across and made the livestock swim. To prepare for river travel, some followed a technique described in a guidebook by Overton Johnson and William Winter, members of the first large wagon train to travel to Oregon in 1843. Their company had gathered a number of fresh buffalo hides, and sewing them together, "stretched them over the wagon beds as tight as [they] could, with the flesh side out, and then turned them up in the sun to dry." They also smeared animal fat and ashes across the hides to waterproof them. With six men to each "boat," they reloaded their goods and ferried them across the mile-wide Platte in multiple trips, a process that took six days. Their patience and planning was rewarded with no accidents or injuries.

Emigrants also worried about the presence of Indians. Many of the pioneers expected the western Indians to be violent, savage people, who randomly attacked wagon trains with tomahawks, war clubs, and bows and arrows. In reality, few attacks occurred during the early years of travel on the Oregon Trail. Native Americans often approached the wagon trains to trade or beg for food and clothing, and they sometimes snuck close to steal horses and cattle. (The tribes felt the emigrants owed them goods for the right to cross their hunting lands.)

"We had no difficulty with the Indians but once. At Fort Hall, the Indians came to our camp and said they wanted to trade. They trade horses for wives. Mr. Bayley joked with them, and asked a young Indian how many horses he would give for [his wife] Caroline. The Indian said, 'Three.' Mr. Bayley said, 'Give me six horses and you can have her,' all in a joke. The next day [the Indian] came after her, and had the six horses, and seemed determined to have her. He followed our wagons for several days, and we were glad to get rid of him without any trouble. . . . Mr. Bayley took good care ever after not to joke with them."

Betsey Bayley, en route from Missouri to Oregon, 1845

In 1847, the governor of Oregon Territory addressed the pioneers' fears and tried to promote peaceful relations in a statement he had posted along the trail. The Indian tribes are "friendly to the whites," he proclaimed, and "should be treated with kindness on all occasions." However, he acknowledged that the Indians were "inclined to steal" and recommended that the emigrants travel "in good-sized companies while passing through their country."

As the Smiths' company moved farther west, the land became more desert-like. By the time they passed the pale cliffs of Scotts Bluff (named for Hiram Scott, a fur trapper who had perished there), the novelty of wagon travel had worn thin. Dry air cracked their lips, and the ground was no longer covered with soft prairie grasses and wildflowers. "The sage is dreadful on one's clothes," Elizabeth complained. "Then there is the prickly pear. Step on it any and everywhere. Look out for bare feet." In addition, a number of people in their wagon train had dysentery, an ailment that causes severe diarrhea.

Near the end of July, the company reached the Sweetwater River and rolled past Independence Rock, a huge mass of granite whose sides were covered with the names of earlier trappers, traders, and pioneers. With her children to feed and keep watch over, Elizabeth had little time to describe the famous rock formations and ever-changing landscape. "Sometimes I would not get the chance to write for two or three days, and then would have to rise in the night when my babe and all hands were asleep, light a candle and write."

Then, August 1, which dawned cold and rainy, the Smiths crossed "the backbone of America"—the Rocky Mountains. Many pioneers were surprised at the gentle grade of South Pass, the sagebrush-covered plain

"Passed Independence Rock. This rock is covered with names. With great difficulty, I found a place to cut mine. Twelve miles from this is Devil's Gate. It's an opening in the mountain through which the Sweetwater River flows. Several of us climbed this mountain—somewhat perilous for youngsters not over fourteen. . . . We were gone so long that the train was stopped and men sent out in search of us. We made all sorts of promises to remain in sight in the future."

Sallie Hester, July 2, 1849

Independence Rock was a favorite trail landmark. Over the years, thousands of pioneers climbed on top of the granite dome for a view of the prairie and left their names scratched or painted in tar on the rock. Farther down the trail, the Sweetwater River flowed between a steep gorge called Devil's Gate.

that led between the towering peaks. Overton Johnson and William Winter remarked in their guidebook, "Both the ascent and descent were so gradual, that, had we not been told, we should have passed over the dividing ridge . . . without knowing it." Nevertheless, the scenery was spectacular. "The lofty summits of the Wind River Mountains, with their wide fields of eternal snow, appeared to be almost beside us." In the high altitude, the weather turned cold, and frost coated the camps with a thin layer of ice by morning.

With their journey half over, the wagons descended from the Rockies, following the Little Sandy, Big Sandy, and Green Rivers. The next stop was Fort Bridger, a ramshackle trading post built by mountain man Jim Bridger and his partner, Louis Vasquez. "This is a pretty place to see in

such a barren country," Elizabeth wrote with relief—"a thousand acres of level land covered with grass, interspersed with beautiful stony brooks, and plenty of timber." Her company rested a few days and bought oxen to replace the ones they had lost. And at long last, Elizabeth and the other women had time to wash their families' dusty, mud-splattered clothing.

On August 22, they reached Soda Springs, where naturally carbonated water bubbled from small mounds in the ground. Previous travelers had described the water as being pleasant to drink, but Elizabeth was unimpressed. "They are not so good as has been represented," she recorded. "Only one or two of our company like it. It tastes like weak vinegar with a little saleratus [baking soda] in it." Finding only one pool that looked clear enough to suit her, she declared they "resemble hog wallows more than springs."

Six days later, they passed the white-washed adobe walls of Fort Hall, a Hudson's Bay Company post. Here a smaller trail branched off to the left—the road to California. But Elizabeth's company aimed toward Oregon on the main branch, entering the desolate Snake River plain during the hottest time of the summer. The livestock suffered for want of water as the wagons passed along the top of the canyon walls. The river flowed

Abandoned wagons became a common sight along trails to the West—left behind by their owners because of a broken axle, tongue, or wheel, or because the oxen pulling them collapsed.

"I used to wonder why it was said that men must be dressed in buckskin to come to this country, but now I know. Everything we travel through is thorny and rough. There is no chance of saving your clothes."

Elizabeth Dixon Smith, October 17, 1847

out of reach far below, and the dirty air crusted the travelers' perspiring faces. "You in 'the States' know nothing about dust," Elizabeth declared in her diary, thinking of her friends in Indiana. "It often seems that the cattle must die for the want of breath, and then in our wagon, such a spectacle—beds, clothes, victuals, and children, all completely covered." While their oxen wheezed and struggled onward, four more members of the exhausted company perished—two men by drowning, and a woman and child to disease. The emigrants had no choice but to bury their loved ones beside the trail.

Almost every wagon train on the Oregon Trail lost at least a few people to sickness or accidents, including misfired guns, drownings, and wagon mishaps. Sometimes people escaped with close calls, such as when a child survived being run over by a wagon during James Fields's 1845 journey. The boy fell from his seat to the ground under the iron-rimmed wagon wheels, which rolled across his chest and arm. "But the ground being soft," Fields recalled, "he was not killed although taken up senseless."

The Smiths' wagon train fared better than many others, but the deaths nonetheless discouraged many of the travelers. In mid-October, after crossing the deep ravines of the Blue Mountains, the company decided to split up. With winter quickly approaching, one group decided to go to the Whitman Mission and wait until spring to complete their journey. Elizabeth's family, however, chose to continue to the Willamette Valley at the end of the trail.

With only a few hundred miles to go, this last leg of the trip would prove by far the hardest. Shivering in the "hard and cold winds," the Smiths braved roads "so narrow that a wagon could hardly squeeze along," and reached the rapid and dangerous Deschutes River. The churning water came clear to the top of the wagon beds, so the women and children used calico shirts to pay two Indians for a canoe ride across while the men struggled with the unhappy animals and precarious wagons. Once safely across, they found the path through the thickly forested Cascade Mountains buried in early winter snows. Unable to pull their wagons any farther, the determined travelers decided to float them down the icy cold Columbia River to the small town of Portland. "Rainy day. Men making

The Cutoff Craze

After several long months on the trail, some pioneers were tempted to take shortcuts, known as cutoffs. More often than not, the routes that sounded too good to be true proved to be just that. In 1845, trying to avoid crossing the difficult Cascade Mountains, a company of about two hundred emigrants followed Stephen Meek, a former fur trapper, on a shortcut south of the Columbia River. By the time the wagon train reached the end of the trail two months later, seventy-five people had died—some from starvation, others poisoned by bad drinking water. Betsey Bayley, one of the survivors, wrote to her sister in Ohio, "We had splendid times until we took what is called 'Meek's Cutoff.' You have no doubt heard of the terrible suffering the people endured on that road."

Despite news of the Meek Party's disastrous shortcut, the very next year, another eager group suffered a similar fate when they tried the untested southern route, a shortcut that swung south from Fort Hall along the Humboldt River and north to Oregon. Along the way, Indians killed a number of their oxen, and a terrible storm hit in October, stranding the group far from help with flooded rivers and icy fogs. Most of the party survived, though it was February before the final members arrived at the Willamette Valley. The governor of Oregon Territory issued a warning to other travelers: "A better way may be found, but it is not best for men with wagons and families to try the experiment."

The most famous story of an ill-fated shortcut was that of the Donner Party, a group of eighty-seven emigrants led by a well-to-do farmer named George Donner and furniture maker James Reed. Tired of bitterly cold Midwest winters, the families planned to settle in sunny California. But rather than taking the established California Trail, which turned off the Oregon Trail farther west at Fort Hall, in 1846, the confident party decided to follow Hastings Cutoff, a new shortcut from Fort Bridger that wound to the south of the Great Salt Lake. They had read the untested route would save them more than three hundred miles. Instead, they found themselves slowed to as little as one mile a day, first by the thick brush and boulder-covered terrain of the Wasatch Mountains, then by the white-hot sun and dry desert land to the west. Almost a hundred of their oxen died of thirst and

James and Margaret Reed, and their daughter Patty, survived the Donner Party disaster in the Sierra Nevada and stayed on to settle in California.

For years after, curious people visited the site where the forlorn families had camped in cabins buried by deep snowdrifts. Sallie Hester, whose family followed the same route as the Donners in 1849, described how "two log cabins, bones of human beings and animals, tops of the trees being cut off the depth of the snow was all that was left to tell the tale of that ill-fated party. . . ." Twenty years later, this California man sat on the same stumps Sallie described.

exhaustion. Quarreling desperately about what to do, the party finally reached Truckee Pass, their final obstacle before descending to Sutter's Fort in the Sacramento Valley. Having camped for five days to let their famished oxen graze in a mountain meadow, the party found themselves caught on the wrong side of the pass when an early blizzard hit. For two weeks, the snow fell thickly, while the group waited anxiously in hastily built cabins and worried about their diminishing food supplies.

Their luck continued downhill. Several times, small groups tried to cross the pass on homemade snowshoes, but deep drifts, thick flurries, and fierce winds blocked their way.

Finally, on January 17, an emaciated man with frozen, bloodied feet, stumbled into Sutter's Fort. William Eddy, and six others who collapsed a few miles back, had survived the horrific trek. Search parties started east with packs of food for the rest of the starving emigrants, but by the time the last survivor was brought out the following spring, forty-four of the eighty-nine members had died. After eating every available scrap of food, including the skin and bones of their cows, and the Donners' pet dog, Cash, the survivors had lived off the flesh of their deceased companions. News of the gruesome tale spread quickly, frightening other wagon trains from attempting untested trails. But the sensational stories discouraged few emigrants from starting west along the main routes. One of the survivors of the Donner Party summed it up best; in a letter to her cousin, teenaged Virginia Reed advised, "Never take no cutoffs and hurry along as fast as you can."

In 1846, Samuel Barlow built a road across the Cascade Mountains on the south side of Mount Hood. For an expensive five-dollar toll, many emigrants chose to avoid the dangerous raft ride that Elizabeth Dixon Smith's family endured, pulling their wagons over Barlow's somewhat-less-dangerous, but steep, mountain highway.

rafts. Women cooking and washing. Children crying. Indians bartering potatoes for shirts," Elizabeth wrote on a dismal November day.

Sharing a forty-foot log raft with two other families, the Smiths took the wheels off their wagon and loaded it on the raft to float down the swirling water. They maneuvered several miles downriver before the water became too rough to continue. Huddled onshore in fiercely blowing winds and rains that never seemed to end, the families waited for a break in the weather. "We clambered up a side hill among the rocks and built a fire and tried to cook and warm ourselves and children," wrote Elizabeth, "while the wind blew and the waves rolled beneath." For a week, the families slowly proceeded, camping on shore under the wet, dripping trees when the river was too rough to travel.

By November 9, their food had run out. With her fingers almost too numb to write, Elizabeth opened her diary to remark, "[This day] finds us still in trouble. Waves dashing over our raft. . . . My husband started this morning to hunt provisions. . . . It is very cold. The icicles are hanging from our wagon beds to the water." The next day, Cornelius returned with fifty pounds of beef loaded on his back, which he had bought from a company farther ahead. Days later, he became sick and delirious with fever. Unable to hold himself upright, Cornelius rode on a mattress in the back of a wagon. "The whole care of everything falls upon my shoulders," Elizabeth scribbled. "I cannot write more at present." She focused on getting her family to Portland, where they could rest and wait out the winter before looking for land to settle.

Traveling part of the way on a washed-out road and hiring a boat to ferry them the final miles, the Smiths at last reached Portland on

"Now I know what none but widows know; that is, how comfortless is that of a widow's life, especially when left in a strange land, without money or friends. . . . "

Elizabeth Dixon Smith, Portland, Oregon, February 2, 1848

Like Elizabeth Dixon Smith, Rachel Fisher Mills suffered tragedy along the Oregon Trail. During the Quaker woman's 1847 trip, her husband, John Fisher, and daughter, Angelina, both died. The twenty-five-year-old widow had little choice but to continue west with her wagon train. By March 1848, she had remarried a young farmer named William Mills, with whom she bore six more children.

November 29. The very next morning, Elizabeth hurried through the muddy streets trying to find shelter for her children and sick husband. The best they could afford was a leaky shack they had to share with two other families. It was so crowded "you could have stirred us with a stick," she described. Selling what few belongings they could spare to pay the rent, they settled in to their damp, crowded home, but Cornelius's health worsened. By the end of January, Elizabeth deplored, "I have not undressed to lie down for six weeks. Besides all our sickness, I had a cross little babe to take care of." The very next day, Cornelius died.

Despite the disastrous end to their journey, with a pioneer's spirit, Elizabeth persevered. On May 25, 1848, a little more than a year after leaving Indiana, she sent the letter her former neighbors had long awaited. "Dear Friends," she began, "By your request I have endeavored to keep a record of our journey from 'the States' to Oregon, though it is poorly done, owing to my having a young babe and . . . a large family to do for. . . ." With mixed emotions—the grief of losing her husband, the pride of having survived, and the homesickness that arose thinking of her distant friends—Elizabeth described her once-in-a-lifetime journey. A few months later, she married Joseph Greer, a jovial, hard-working man from Illinois, whose first wife had also died soon after arriving in Oregon. The new couple settled down with their children and planted a large orchard of pear and apple trees. As Joseph described, "We are not rich, but independent, and live agreeably together, which is enough. We are located on the west bank of the Willamette River about twenty miles above Oregon City . . . a very pleasant situation." ❂

7

The Road
to Zion

Pioneering the Mormon Trail

With prairie grasses brushing against his legs, William Clayton plodded slowly next to his wagon, his eyes fixed on one of the large, wooden wheels. His joints ached with rheumatism and his brow dripped with sweat, but the thirty-two-year-old clerk painstakingly counted each turn of the wagon wheel. He had measured the wheel's circumference and knew it was exactly fourteen feet eight inches. For every 360 turns of the wheel, the wagon train traveled one mile. With this system of careful counting, he would know exactly how far they progressed each day.

Clayton wanted to be precise because he was recording the information for future travelers, and he was sure his companions had been overestimating their mileage. Often, he used his journal to vent frustrations. "The reason why I have taken this method, which is somewhat tedious," he wrote, "is because there is generally a difference of two and sometimes four miles in a day's travel between my estimation and that of some others, and they have all thought I underrated it."

Clayton also kept detailed descriptions of the route and the landscape, recording a few lines each day, such as "Elk Horn [River], nine rods wide, three feet deep. Current rather swift, and not very pleasant to ferry," or "Long Lake, south side [of] the road. There is a little timber where this lake joins the river, and it is a good camping place." He wanted to tell those who followed where to find wood for their campfires and water for themselves and their oxen. They would also need to know the

William Clayton's Overland Journal

April 26, 1847

"This morning about 3:30 an alarm was sounded. I immediately got out of the wagon and learned that three of the guard who were stationed to the northeast of the camp had discovered some Indians crawling up towards the wagons. They first received alarm from the motions of one of our horses, . . . and listening, heard something rustle in the grass; they first suspected they were wolves and fired at them. Only one gun went off and six Indians sprang up and ran from within a few rods of where they stood. . . . After daylight the footsteps of the Indians could be plainly seen where they had come down under the bank and sometimes stepped into the water. No doubt their object was to steal horses. . . .

"President Young, Kimball, G. A. Smith, A. Lyman, and others went ahead on horseback to point out the road. The horse teams traveled first to break the strong grass so that it will not hurt the oxen's feet. The hunters started out in different directions keeping only a few miles from the wagons. . . . From this place . . . can be seen the remains of an old village or Indian fort. . . . The country looks beautiful, somewhat rolling and bounded by uneven bluffs. The land looks poor and sandy. The sun is very hot and not much wind. I find it has a great tendency to make sore lips, parched up and feverish."

April 30, 1847

"After supper I went and gathered some dried buffalo dung (politely called buffalo chips) to cook with in the morning. Brother Hanson played some on his violin and some

Like many pioneers, William Clayton recorded countless details and anecdotes in his journal. The trip overland, for Mormons and non-Mormons alike, would prove one of the most memorable experiences of their lives.

of the brethren danced to warm themselves. I went to bed early to get warm but having only one quilt for covering, I suffered much with cold."

May 6, 1847

"We have never been out of sight of herds of buffalo today, and from where we are camped, I am satisfied we can see over five thousand with the glass. The largest herd we have yet seen is still ahead of us. The prairie looks black with them, both on this and the other side of the river. Some think we have passed fifty, and some even a hundred thousand during the day. . . . It is truly a sight wonderful to behold. . . . "

May 9, 1847

"We arrived here at nine-fifty and shall stay until morning. Soon as the camp was formed, I went about three quarters of a mile below to the river and washed my socks, towel, and handkerchief as well as I could in cold water without soap. I then stripped my clothing off and washed from head to foot, which has made me feel much more comfortable for I was covered with dust. After washing and putting on clean clothing, I sat down on the banks of the river and gave way to a long train of solemn reflections respecting many things, especially in regard to my family and their welfare for time and eternity."

safest places to cross streams and rivers, and the number of miles they should be prepared to travel on a given day.

It was 1847, and Clayton and his companions had left their homes on the Missouri frontier to cross the western prairies. Unlike the estimated four thousand pioneers who were spread out over the twisting route of the Oregon Trail along the south bank of the Platte River, Clayton's seventy-three-wagon party had chosen to travel along the river's north bank. And while the other emigrants aimed for the fertile river valleys of western Oregon or the sunny climate of coastal California, his group was unsure of its final destination.

Clayton and his fellow travelers belonged to the Church of Jesus Christ of Latter-day Saints, also known as the Mormon Church. Founded in 1830 by a New York farmhand named Joseph Smith, the church had been based in Kirtland, Ohio, then Independence, Missouri, and finally the town of Nauvoo, Illinois. At each location, non-Mormons had forced the Saints, as the members called themselves, to leave.

It was a time of sweeping religious reform, and many people, including Joseph Smith, were questioning established religions or breaking away to start new churches. But the majority of Americans held on to more traditional beliefs, and they viewed the reformers as radicals. Violence often resulted as each group passionately defended its religion. Smith's controversial Mormon Church suffered more intense persecution than most, partly because of its unusual history.

In 1823, the teenaged Smith said that, with the help of an angel, he had found a set of fourteen-hundred-year-old golden tablets buried in a field. Engraved on them was a story about a group of Israelites who sailed to North America and built a flourishing civilization. The young visionary based his new religion on those mysterious writings. He published a translation of the text, called the Book of Mormon, but refused to show the actual tablets to any but his closest believers. Some people called the story an outrageous hoax, but Smith quickly gained many followers. To avoid criticism, the Mormons isolated themselves in tightly knit communities. Converts followed strict laws established by Smith and donated much of

The Mormon faith required converts to consider the good of the group before individual needs. In return for their obedience, the Saints received the spiritual and economic support of the community and, they believed, entrance to heaven. To many families, the church offered an escape from poverty.

their earnings to the church. In return for their obedience, they could rely on the moral and financial support of the church. But everywhere the Saints tried to settle, non-Mormons harassed them, forcing them to move on.

In Nauvoo, as the Mormon population grew to more than twenty thousand people, the non-Mormons became increasingly uneasy. To make matters worse, news leaked out that Smith supported polygamy—the controversial practice of a man having more than one wife at a time. The tense situation erupted in June 1844, when an angry mob of Illinois settlers killed Smith and his brother Hyrum, hoping the leader's death would cause the downfall of the hated church. Instead, the tragedy further united the members, and a new leader emerged— charismatic, strong-willed Brigham Young. Seeing no chance for a peaceful existence in Illinois, the former Vermont resident turned his followers' hopes to the West. Somewhere in the wilderness, on the other side of the Rocky Mountains, the Saints would build a new community— a promised land where they could practice their faith without criticism or fear of assault.

Beginning in February 1846, Young and more than

Brigham Young, pictured here in the late 1840s, held absolute power in the Mormon Church. When he discovered his followers bickering among themselves, the fearless leader delivered fiery speeches reminding the Saints of their sacred duties. Young made a point of paying attention to detail; he was able to address thousands of Mormons by their first names.

In 1846, after five years of constant labor, the Saints had nearly completed construction of a magnificent limestone temple on a hilltop overlooking Nauvoo. The day after the building was dedicated, the Mormons had to abandon it as they fled to the Salt Lake Valley.

In February 1846, when Brigham Young led the first emigrants out of Nauvoo, the Mississippi River was full of floating ice. Within days, the river froze over completely, allowing the Saints to cross on top of the ice.

fifteen thousand Mormons fled Nauvoo in strings of wagon trains, crossing the Mississippi River into Iowa. They built a temporary village, called Winter Quarters, west of Council Bluffs on the Missouri River. The following spring, while the others waited in camp, Young led a scouting party west to search for the exact site of their promised land, which they called Zion. Church clerk William Clayton was among this group of 143 men, which also included 3 women and 2 young boys, as well as 19 cows, 17 dogs, and a number of chickens.

When Clayton tired of counting wagon wheel revolutions, he asked a mechanic named Appleton Harmon to help him design a device he called a roadometer. Harmon carefully whittled the wooden instrument and installed it on the wagon hub. Every six revolutions, the wheel twisted a screwlike device around once, which in turn pushed on a small wheel with sixty teeth. For every full revolution of the sixty-toothed wheel, the wagon had traveled one mile. Another small screw pushed on a thirty-toothed wheel that counted each mile. Clayton could now concentrate on writing descriptions of the timber, water sources, weather, and wildlife they encountered. He also helped the other men dislodge wagons that got stuck in sandy streambeds or muddy patches in the trail. And at the end of each day, Clayton erected a sign stating their mileage and giving directions for the others at Winter Quarters to follow.

On June 27, after eleven grueling weeks, the group crossed the Continental Divide at South Pass. By this time, Brigham Young had decided where he was leading his people. He had become intrigued by a place in the western Rockies called the valley of the Great Salt Lake,

"I got a small board and wrote on it: 'From Winter Quarters three hundred miles, May 9, 1847. Pioneer Camp all well. Distance according to the reckoning of Wm. Clayton.' This was nailed on a post and in the evening I went and set it up about three hundred yards from here on a bend of the river."

William Clayton, May 9, 1847

which army explorer John Charles Frémont described as having "valuable, nutritious grass" and access to trees and water in the foothills. But a grizzled old mountain man named Moses "Black" Harris told Young that the information was wrong. The valley, he said, was "sandy and destitute of timber and vegetation except the wild sage." Still, Young and his followers weren't dissuaded. Clayton noted in his journal, "We

More than fifteen thousand Saints made their way to Winter Quarters. In the temporary camp, four hundred miles west of Nauvoo on the Missouri River, they patiently waited for instructions from Young and prepared for a journey to the yet-unknown promised land. During the winter, supplies of food and fuel ran low, and more than six hundred men, women, and children died of cholera and other diseases. Still, few people deserted.

Young and the other Mormon leaders carefully read the works of army explorer John Charles Frémont, who traveled extensively through the West during the early 1840s. Frémont's descriptions, which often exaggerated the riches of the land, inspired the Mormons to try settling the remote Salt Lake Valley.

generally feel that we shall know best by going ourselves for the reports of travelers are so contradictory it is impossible to know which is the truth without going to prove it."

The very next day, Young had a chance to question another experienced Rocky Mountain traveler—Jim Bridger. He, too, tried to discourage them, warning of a steep mountain range tangled with vegetation that they would have to cross to reach the valley. And although he said he knew of Indian tribes who grew wheat and other crops in some sections of the valley, the trapper jested that he would give the Mormon pioneers a thousand dollars if they could raise one bushel of corn in that flat expanse of bunch grasses and hard-packed soil.

But Young stubbornly believed that, with hard work and good planning, the Mormons could succeed in the inhospitable land, which at the time was officially part of Mexican territory. And if others considered it undesirable, then the Saints could finally live and work undisturbed.

Near Bridger's trading fort, the Saints turned off the Oregon Trail to the southwest, following the same path the unlucky Donner Party had struggled over one year earlier before they were trapped by blizzards in the Sierra Nevada. Clayton and the other men found the Wasatch Mountains to be as difficult as Bridger had cautioned. Thick brush, matted willow trees, and boulders blocked their way on the steep canyon trail. Many of them suffered from "mountain fever," a mysterious illness that caused high fevers, severe headaches, and aching joints. Under the glaring sun, with grim determination—and nightly prayers to remind them of their goal—the Saints pushed on.

On July 22, two scouts shouted for joy

The desert-like Salt Lake Valley offered poor hunting. Few game animals could survive the harsh climate, but rattlesnakes, horned toads, and crickets abounded.

as they caught sight of the Great Salt Lake, shimmering in the searing sunlight. Two days later, the Mormon leader had his first glimpse of the broad valley—lush for the moment with summer grasses and sparkling with small creeks that flowed from the mountains. From the back of a wagon bed, where he, too, was fighting off mountain fever, Young sat up and declared they had reached the end of the trail. This was Zion. Here, in this uninhabited valley, surrounded by miles of mountains and desert, they would build a city and live in peace. Clayton imagined how different the Saints' lives would be in the isolated mountain valley.

> ## Farewell to the Land of My Birth
>
> *I go where no tyrants dare come,*
> *Where oppressors would tremble to tread,*
> *Where the honest in heart find a home,*
> *Where the blessings of heaven are shed.*
>
> *'Tis with joy I am bidding farewell*
> *To the proud, boasted land of my birth;*
> *I go with the upright to dwell,*
> *Where the pure will find heaven on earth.*
>
> *It is Faith, 'tis not fancy, that paints*
> *The vision of bliss that I see,*
> *I go to the home of the Saints—*
> *To Zion, the land of the Free.*
>
> **By Ann Cash**

Despite his worries, he had no doubt that he would rather live "in this wild-looking country" than back East where the Saints were "eternally mobbed, harassed, hunted, our best men murdered, and every good man's life [was] continually in danger."

The minute the wagons pulled to a halt on the valley floor, the men unloaded their plows to break the ground. Within days, they had flooded fifty acres of the sun-baked earth to soften the soil and planted crops of corn, potatoes, oats, and beans. Once the seeds were in the ground, the men opened a road to a canyon seven miles away, where they could chop down pine and fir trees and haul back logs. They also marked off streets in the gritty dirt, according to a city plan Young mapped out, and began building homes of logs and adobe.

Yet no sooner had the men reached the promised land than it was time for many of them, including William Clayton, to leave. Fifteen hundred Mormon pioneers were faithfully following the advance party's trail markings and would soon be arriving in the Salt Lake Valley to bolster the work efforts. But back at Winter Quarters, thirteen thousand Saints remained, waiting for instructions on when and where to proceed.

On August 17, Clayton and a small troop of men turned their ox-drawn wagons eastward. Along the way, they passed the first incoming bands of emigrants and shared the joyful news that Zion was ready

"When I think of the many dangers from accident which families traveling this road are continually liable to . . . it makes me almost shudder to think of it and I could almost envy those who have got safely through, having their families with them, yet they will doubtless have a hard time of it the coming winter."

William Clayton, Salt Lake Valley, July 22, 1847

and waiting for them. Clayton carefully retraced their steps, adding to his original notes and using a new roadometer to confirm the distances from point to point along the trail. Nine weeks later, he was back at Winter Quarters, greeting his wife, Diantha, and a new baby that had been born while he was away.

The Saints' work had only begun. The first winter in their promised land brought frigid temperatures and near starvation; their first year's crops had done poorly, and the harvests were disappointingly small. But the settlers poured their energy into damming mountain streams and digging

Salt Lake City, pictured here in 1853, is surrounded by peaks that rise more than seven thousand feet from the valley floor.

miles of irrigation ditches, channeling the water to newly tilled fields. Slowly they transformed the flat, dry valley into productive farmland. Rather than the typical frontier mentality of each man for himself, the Mormons worked as a group to establish themselves. Their joint determination allowed them to succeed where other emigrants never would have considered settling.

The following year, twenty-four hundred more Saints traveled to Zion, where a small, neatly planned city of wood and adobe houses stood on the valley floor. When they started on the trail that spring, the second migration of Mormon pioneers had an excellent guide in their hands:

THE

LATTER-DAY SAINTS'
EMIGRANTS' GUIDE:

BEING A

TABLE OF DISTANCES,

SHOWING ALL THE

SPRINGS, CREEKS, RIVERS, HILLS, MOUNTAINS, CAMPING PLACES, AND ALL OTHER NOTABLE PLACES,

FROM COUNCIL BLUFFS

TO THE

VALLEY OF THE GREAT SALT LAKE.

ALSO, THE

LATITUDES, LONGITUDES, AND ALTITUDES OF THE PROMINENT POINTS ON THE ROUTE.

TOGETHER WITH REMARKS ON THE NATURE OF THE LAND, TIMBER, GRASS, &c.

THE WHOLE ROUTE HAVING BEEN CAREFULLY MEASURED BY A ROADOMETER, AND THE DISTANCE FROM POINT TO POINT, IN ENGLISH MILES, ACCURATELY SHOWN.

BY W. CLAYTON.

The Latter-day Saints' Emigrants' Guide by William Clayton.

The Saints had followed Young across the Mississippi into the western wilderness to find "a home . . . where they would be free from persecution." But despite their success in taming the land in the Salt Lake Valley, other obstacles awaited them. In 1848, after the Mexican War, the valley became part of the United States, and all too soon, the Mormons were fighting battles similar to those they had encountered in Illinois, Missouri, and Ohio. Following the discovery of gold in California, thousands of prospectors passed through Salt Lake City on their way west, dashing the Mormons' hopes for isolation. This time, though, the Saints had dug in their heels deep enough that they would never be forced to move again. ✪

8

From Texas to California

The War with Mexico

WHILE AMERICAN TRAPPERS, missionaries, and pioneers blazed routes through Louisiana Territory and into Oregon, great changes were occurring in the Southwest. After almost three hundred years of Spanish rule, in 1821, Mexico won its independence. Free from Spain's colonial grasp, the new government immediately lifted the strict policies that had prevented Mexicans from trading with Americans. Before the year ended, Missouri trader William Becknell and five companions had ventured to the once-off-limits town of Santa Fe. The adobe village had long been a trading site for Mexicans and Native Americans such as the Pueblo Indians. Becknell's group excitedly discovered that their small stash of dry goods could be sold for tremendous profits. Riding away with their rawhide sacks bulging with silver pesos, they quickly headed across the dry plains and grassy prairies to Missouri and outfitted a much larger caravan of goods.

A brisk new trade developed. From the Missouri frontier, American merchants traveled west in sturdy freight wagons brimming with bolts of cloth, leather shoes, metal tools, and glassware. And Mexican traders headed east carrying packs of furs and silver, and driving herds of half-wild mules and horses to sell in Missouri. Both countries benefited from the open exchange of goods. Traffic on the eight-hundred-mile route, known as the Santa Fe Trail, increased each year. Unlike the Oregon Trail, the route to New Mexico was used by merchants traveling back and forth to sell their goods, not by pioneer families in search of a new

A group of Mexican traders load their mules with heavy packs of goods during the heyday of the Santa Fe Trail. The mule drivers, or arrieros, often used untamed animals to carry their goods over the difficult trail. To calm the frantic ones while they packed, the men tied blindfolds over the mules' eyes.

home. Still, through the stories of Santa Fe Trail travelers, Americans became aware that Mexico's remote northwestern frontier offered many opportunities.

In the northeast of Mexico, relations with the United States developed differently. The same year Mexico became independent, a twenty-seven-year-old Missouri resident named Stephen Austin received permission to settle three hundred American families in Texas. Mexico required the immigrants to become Mexican citizens and to convert to Catholicism, the national religion. The government hoped that Austin's colony of farmers, cotton growers, and ranchers would help bring order to the wild northern land. Until then, Texas had been inhabited by only a few thousand Spanish settlers and widely scattered Native American tribes. Attracted by the promise of free land, the Americans agreed to the terms.

Austin's settlers established several small towns along the Brazos River, where they built wood-frame houses and barns, marked their lands with split-rail fences, and imported equipment and goods from New Orleans. They were so successful that other Americans joined them. Soon the flood of immigrants into Texas began to alarm the Mexican government. Many of the settlers came legally, but hundreds came as squatters

When Stephen Austin started his Texas colony, he was following a path begun by his father. Moses Austin had successfully petitioned the Spanish government for a land grant in 1821, but he died before the arrangements were completed. Stephen carried through with his father's plans and selected a site along the lower reaches of the Colorado and Brazos Rivers. Of the eighteen hundred original settlers in his colony, more than four hundred were slaves. The Mexican Congress wanted to outlaw slavery, but Austin negotiated a compromise: The American Texans could import slaves, but not sell them, and at the age of fourteen, slave children would automatically earn their freedom.

looking for free land and criminals hoping to escape the American justice system. To regain control, in 1830, the Mexican dictator General Antonio López de Santa Anna banned further American immigration into Texas and imposed high taxes on the established settlers.

Residents of the remote Texan towns refused to recognize Santa Anna's new laws, just as they had ignored Mexican laws and taxes in the past. Living nearly eight hundred miles from the national government in Mexico City, across more than a dozen rivers, deep canyons, desolate mountains, and arid deserts, the farmers and ranchers had always followed their own rules. In addition, the former Americans complained that the Mexican

government didn't provide needed facilities such as roads, public schools, and post offices. "Why should we pay taxes if the money isn't spent on us?" they argued.

To force the settlers to cooperate, the fiercely proud Santa Anna sent troops to enforce the new laws, but his plan backfired. In the fall of 1835, the Texans rebelled, capturing the towns of San Antonio and Gonzales from Mexico. They declared they were fighting for restoration of the Mexican constitution of 1824, which Santa Anna had overthrown. But by March 1836, the Texans voted to fight for independence instead. With only a small volunteer army, they had their work cut out for them. That same month, a powerful Mexican army of 6,000 seasoned soldiers reached Texas. In San Antonio, the troops slaughtered more than 180 Texans who desperately tried to defend the Alamo, an abandoned mission building they had garrisoned. But the bloody defeat further united the rebels, inspiring them to continue the fight to break away from Mexico. On April 21, they had their revenge. Led by rough-and-tumble General Sam Houston, the small Texan army surprised Santa Anna's troops at their camp on the San Jacinto River during their afternoon siesta. The Mexican general had thought the outnumbered Texan army wouldn't dare attack his camp.

Armed with handguns and bowie knives, the eight hundred Texans crept close before charging in with bloodcurdling yells. The brutal, hand-to-hand fighting lasted only twenty minutes. Losing fewer than ten men, Houston's army killed some six hundred Mexicans and captured seven hundred prisoners—including Santa Anna himself. Houston quickly negotiated a deal with the defeated Mexican leader: He would spare his life and those of his troops if they retreated immediately from Texas. Santa Anna agreed to the terms and fled to his home in Vera Cruz. Sam Houston was elected president of the new country, which the Texans called the Lone Star Republic.

The Texans had earned their freedom, but the Lone Star Republic lacked the money to build a government or strengthen its army. And Mexico continued to threaten new attacks,

After a thirteen-day siege, Santa Anna ordered his troops to storm the Alamo on the morning of March 6. The small force of Texans who died in the bloody battle included the well-known frontiersmen Jim Bowie and Davy Crockett.

The town of Austin, one of the first settlements established by Stephen Austin's colonists, was selected capital of the Republic of Texas in 1839.

despite a rapid turnover of leaders following Santa Anna's downfall. Worried they wouldn't be able to maintain independence for long, the Texans voted to apply for annexation to the United States.

The admittance of Texas as a new state posed serious difficulties for Congress, which was embroiled over the issue of slavery. Almost all Texans had originally come from southern states where slavery was legal, and many continued to own slaves. If the Lone Star Republic were

Samuel Houston, who led Texan troops to victory at the Battle of San Jacinto, became the first president of the Republic of Texas in 1836.

For a military hero and politician, Houston had a unique past. During his childhood in Tennessee, he had spent time with nearby Cherokee Indians and learned their language and customs. Eventually Houston became governor of the state, but when his wife left him in 1829, he resigned his post and went to live with Cherokee Indians in Arkansas. Then, while traveling as a spokesman for the Indians, he wound up in Texas and decided to remain. Following the annexation of Texas into the Union, Houston served as U.S. senator for fourteen years before being elected governor of Texas in 1859.

> *"Victory is certain. Trust in God and fear not. And remember the Alamo! Remember the Alamo!"*
>
> **General Sam Houston, to his Texan troops,
> prior to the Battle of San Jacinto, April 21, 1836**

admitted to the Union, supporters of slavery would gain political power, which caused anti-slavery congressmen to raise strong objections. For nine years, Americans argued about whether to admit Texas; finally, in 1845, it became the twenty-eighth state.

Mexico had repeatedly warned the United States that it still considered the rebellious Texas to be part of its country, and if the Americans admitted Texas as a state, it would be considered an act of war. Although Mexico didn't really want to fight its powerful neighbor, an additional dispute provoked it to the point of no return. For years, Mexicans had accepted the southern border of Texas to be the Nueces River. Now the American government claimed the border was 150 miles to the south at the Rio Grande River. Still trying to

*The Mexican government disputed
Santa Anna's cowardly terms of surrender after the Battle of
San Jacinto. Instead of risking his life for his country and calling for
additional Mexican troops, the general had agreed to make a quick retreat.*

Many Americans opposed the war with Mexico. Abolitionists, people who wanted to end slavery in America, saw it as an attempt by Southerners to extend slavery. Others viewed President Polk's actions as immoral land-grabbing.

THE TRIBUNE.

From our Extra of Yesterday Morning.

BY ELECTRIC TELEGRAPH!

CABINET AT WASHINGTON CONVENED ON SUNDAY MORNING.

50,000 VOLUNTEERS CALLED FOR!

$10,000,000 TO BE RAISED!

Additional and important particulars of War with Mexico !!!

avoid a bloody conflict, Mexico decided it wouldn't take action unless the Americans actually crossed the Nueces.

That fall, President James K. Polk sent a congressman named John Slidell on a secret mission to Mexico City to negotiate the disputed border and to offer to purchase New Mexico and California for $30 million. When Mexican officials refused to receive Slidell, Polk responded to the snub with a taunt: He ordered General Zachary Taylor to move his army into the disputed land between the Nueces and Rio Grande Rivers. For five months, the Mexicans refrained from attacking. On May 9, 1846, the fed-up Polk was preparing a pro-war speech to deliver to Congress, when he received news that Mexican troops had crossed the Rio Grande on April 25 and, at long last, attacked Taylor's troops, killing or injuring sixteen men. The president quickly rewrote his speech with fiery, patriotic language. Mexico had invaded U.S. territory, he declared, and "shed American blood on American soil." Congress overwhelmingly approved the declaration of war.

A thousand miles from Texas, in Mexico's province of California, other troubles had surfaced. Early in the morning of June 14, Mexican General Mariano Vallejo was awakened at his home in Sonoma by the clattering of horses' hooves and a loud knocking at his door. Vallejo, the military commander of the region north of San Francisco, was no longer on active duty and had no troops under his command, but a few dozen land-hungry Americans arrested him and occupied the town. Despite the fact that only about seven hundred Americans lived in California (compared to ten thousand Mexicans), the

President James K. Polk had ambitious expansion plans for the United States. He believed Mexico would try to avoid war with a country that had twice its population and enough money in its treasury to build a large army.

"To fit regular troops for so long a march is a great undertaking, but to equip and put in fighting order . . . volunteers, all of whom (even the officers) being ignorant of their duties, is a task requiring a large stock of patience."

**Lieutenant Abraham Robinson Johnston, preparing to leave
Fort Leavenworth for Santa Fe, June 30, 1846**

rebels issued a declaration of independence, naming their "country" the Bear Flag Republic. A few weeks later, amid the turmoil, the Californians finally received news of the war with Mexico. The Bear Flaggers gave up their reckless fight for independence and sided with the United States. Suddenly Mexico was in danger of losing all of its northern lands, from the Gulf of Mexico to the coast of the Pacific—a total of half its territory.

While General Taylor's men continued to invade Mexico south of the Rio Grande, General Stephen Kearny marched troops—known as the Army of the West—to New Mexico and California. Many of Kearny's men were volunteers who had excitedly answered the president's call to arms that spring. Having rushed to represent their country in the war, the inexperienced soldiers soon found life in the field to be hard work.

Eighteen-year-old Marcellus Ball Edwards, who worked as a clerk for Saline County, Missouri, enlisted as a private soon after the war began. On June 23, less than three weeks after setting off for New Mexico, the mounted volunteer recorded in his journal: "After completing ten miles and in the midst of a very heavy rain, we unsaddled, picketed our horses on the grass, and pitched our tents. Everything being wet and the rain unceasing, it was impossible to kindle a fire. So we were in a pretty bad fix and had to grin and bear it." Just three days later, the rainstorm had long blown away, and Edwards wrote, "This day's march has been over the most destitute country I've ever seen, the grass scarce, short, scorched, and in fact, almost burnt to a cinder by the heat of the sun. . . ."

In addition to the extremes of weather they encountered on the prairies and deserts of the Southwest, Edwards learned that the farther the troops traveled, the less they could rely on the army for regular shipments of food or supplies of water. On August 9, with his stomach grumbling, he jotted in his journal, "This is a day that will be long and painfully recollected by every member of the Army of the West. The men, who had nothing to eat yesterday, got nothing until late in the evening [today]." When the rations finally arrived, Edwards and his companions unhappily discovered, "It was simply . . . flour at the rate of one half pint per day . . . with some beef that was so poor and tough that it was blue."

"This day's march is one . . . that never shall be forgotten. The heat of the sun was suffocating, while the dust rose in clouds in our ranks. . . . No water was met with to quench the burning thirst occasioned by this until near night … and this [was] so bad that one who drank it would have to shut both eyes and hold his breath until the nauseating dose was swallowed. Notwithstanding its scarcity, some men allowed their horses to tramp through [the water], which soon stirred it up to a thick mud, and—to give it still greater flavor—a dead snake with the flesh just dropping from its bones."

Private Marcellus Ball Edwards, August 4, 1846

Aside from the hardships of the long march, General Kearny's troops met no organized resistance from the people of New Mexico, who lived far north of the heart of the country and received little support from the Mexican army. He sent messengers in advance to deliver a proclamation to the Mexicans and Native Americans, stating "that if they will remain neutral, stay at home, and attend to their peaceful and respective occupations, their lives, property, rights, etc., would be protected and respected by the American army."

On August 18, Kearny claimed Santa Fe, the capital of the province, for the United States. As one soldier recalled, "Before the sun went down, the Star-Spangled Banner, hoisted amid the noise of a federal salute, was waving from the abandoned mansions of the late governor of New Mexico." That evening, Private Edwards described seeing Mexican women "with their hands covering their faces or sobbing aloud," distraught at the sight of foreign soldiers in their streets. Following their success in New Mexico, Edwards and many of his fellow Missouri volunteers began a march led by Colonel Alexander Doniphan along the upper reaches of the Rio Grande and through the rugged Mexican countryside to join Zachary Taylor's army. Known as Doniphan's expedition, the small Missouri force single-handedly conquered the state of Chihuahua and became instant heroes in the American press.

South of the disputed Texas border, General Taylor's troops were meeting the brunt of

General Zachary Taylor returned home from Mexico a national hero. Soon after the war, he was elected the twelfth president of the United States.

Captain Ephraim Kirby Smith, who fought in the battles of Palo Alto and Resaca de la Palma under General Taylor's command, and at Vera Cruz and Churubusco for General Scott, wrote numerous letters to his wife describing his experiences in Mexico.

March 17, 1846, Filisolas Wells

An express came to us here from General Taylor announcing "The enemy is on our front, threatening to attack us if we advance." . . . We were all much excited and forgot our fatigues and sufferings and discussed our prospects around our camp fires. . . . I got some sleep this night and rose much refreshed at two in the morning when our reveille sounded. . . . We made this day a long march over a perfect desert, the scanty herbage having been burnt by the enemy. The only water we saw was salt and the sun streamed upon us like living fire.

May 13, 1846, At our old camp opposite Matamoras

On the eighth, as I anticipated, we met the enemy on the prairie and fought them five hours—whipping them severely. . . . The cannonade continued until night closed in when the spectacle was magnificent. The prairie was burning brilliantly between the two armies and some twenty pieces of artillery thundering from right to left, while through the lurid scene was heard the tramping of horses and the wild cheering of men. . . . The enemy suffered horribly.

November 23, 1846, Saltillo

The intelligent portion of the Mexican population are of the opinion, and express it to us without reserve, that the war is wicked and aggressive on the part of the United States.

January 27, 1847, Camp Palo Alto

A few words in apology for my journal. It has been written from day to day with a stump of a pencil, often on my knee in my tent at night after a fatiguing march, when I was cold, weary, and disgusted with everything in this miserable world.

August 22, 1847, Tacubaya

I hardly know how to commence a description of the events of the last three days. My brain is whirling from the long continued excitement and my body sore with bruises and fatigue. . . . The din was most horrible, the roar of cannon and musketry, the screams of the wounded, the awful cry of terrified horses and mules, and the yells of the fierce combatants all combined in a sound as hellish as can be conceived.

On September 7, outside the gates of Mexico City, Smith solemnly wrote, "Tomorrow will be a day of slaughter. I firmly trust and pray that victory may crown our efforts though the odds are immense. I am thankful that you do not know the peril we are in. Good night." Early the next morning, he was shot in the face at the Battle of Molino del Ray. Without regaining consciousness, Smith died three days later—less than a week before Scott's army captured the city.

On February 23, 1847, General Taylor's 4,759 officers and men forced 20,000 Mexican troops to retreat from the country's interior mountains in the Battle of Buena Vista.

Outside the gates of Mexico City stood Chapultepec Palace, known as the Halls of Montezuma. The grand building had loomed over the city since the early 1500s, during the reign of the last Aztec emperor, Montezuma. In 1847, the palace housed Mexico's National Military Academy—the final stronghold Scott's army had to defeat before entering the capital.

General Winfield Scott, who earned the nickname "Old Fuss and Feathers" for his emphasis on military formalities, paraded his victorious troops into Mexico City on September 14, 1847.

Below: When the terms of peace were announced, Mexican citizens living within the new American boundaries had the choice of moving south or becoming United States citizens. The thousands who chose to remain had to adapt to a new language and to the laws and customs of a vastly different culture.

the Mexican forces. The United States emerged victorious from all of the major battles, but not without casualties. With no immediate end to the war in sight, President Polk ordered General Winfield Scott to mount an additional campaign—taking an army by sea to the port city of Vera Cruz on the eastern coast of Mexico. Scott had orders to capture it, and, leaving no doubt as to who was in control, march inland and capture Mexico's capital city. After days of heavy bombardment, Vera Cruz surrendered. Over the next six months, Scott's troops fought their way to Mexico City, which they finally invaded September 13, 1847.

TREATY
OF
PEACE, FRIENDSHIP, LIMITS,
AND
SETTLEMENT,
BETWEEN THE
UNITED STATES OF AMERICA
AND THE
MEXICAN REPUBLIC,
Concluded at Guadalupe Hidalgo, February 2, and Ratified, with the Amendments, by the American Senate, March 10, 1848.

Brought to its knees by the fall of the national capital, on February 2, 1848, Mexico signed the Treaty of Guadalupe Hidalgo, officially ending the war. In the treaty, Mexico accepted the Rio Grande as the southern border of Texas and ceded the provinces of New Mexico and California to the United States for $15 million. (The huge land cession encompassed the present-day states of California, New Mexico, Nevada, Utah, and Arizona as well as parts of Colorado and Wyoming.) In just three years—since the annexation of Texas in 1845 and the acquisition of Oregon in 1846—the United States had almost doubled in size. And, for the first time, the country stretched across the continent, from the Atlantic Coast to the Pacific Coast. ✪

9
Gold!

The Forty-niners

DR. BENJAMIN CORY didn't want to practice medicine anymore. In the past six months, since word had spread of the flecks and nuggets of sparkling metal found at Sutter's Mill in the Coloma Valley, almost every man in northern California had fled for the foothills of the Sierra Nevada. Why, Dr. Cory asked himself, should he bother tending patients for the paltry sum of a few dollars a visit, when he could make several thousand dollars a month panning for gold?

But even at his camp in the mountains, people continued to pester the reluctant doctor for medical services, so he devised a plan to discourage them. "I will visit no patient for less than an ounce of gold," he wrote his brother, "unless it is a rare case—a case of poverty." Dr. Cory admitted the mining life he had chosen was not easy. "I have lived somewhat roughly here in the mountains. . . . I have frequently had to cook my bread and meat upon a stick or in the ashes." Still, the life outdoors suited him. "I have gotten so that wherever night overtakes me, I feel as if I were in my house. I sleep as well on the hard ground, with perhaps a root or stone under my ribs, as if I were in the softest bed."

It was November 1848, and California was the talk of the nation. Early that year, the United States had obtained the once-quiet frontier land from Mexico. The coastal territory had been sparsely populated by a varied mix of people—Mexican cattle ranchers and their employees, numerous Indian tribes, American settlers, and a smattering of foreigners. Trading ships that sailed into the tiny port towns of San Diego, Los

The life of a miner was often extremely lonely. One young prospector complained, "I have nothing to read, no friends to visit. My only pastime is eating, sleeping, walking, and occasionally writing, but letter writing is a bore; besides it is useless to write to the States as I never receive any answers to my letters."

Angeles, and San Francisco brought people from the eastern United States, England, France, Russia, Germany, and the Sandwich Islands. And since 1841, wagon trains of pioneers from western states such as Iowa and Missouri had struggled over the desolate Southwest deserts and treacherous passes of the Sierra Nevada.

Among these California settlers, a Swiss emigrant named John Augustus Sutter had built a fifty-thousand-acre empire in the Sacramento Valley from a Mexican land grant he received in 1840. He hired a number of local Indians to raise crops of wheat, run a mercantile store and blacksmith shop, and tend large herds of cattle, horses, and sheep.

On a cool January day, eight years after acquiring his land, Sutter's life took an abrupt turn. While overseeing the building of a new sawmill on the American River, mill boss James Marshall caught a glimpse of yellowish metal among the coarse gravel, sand, and mud where the river had been channeled toward the mill wheel. He bent and picked out several pale lumps, examining them more closely in his fingers. With his heart beating faster and faster, he tested the pieces by pounding them between two rocks. They dented but didn't break. The mill boss was no expert, but he was sure this was gold! A few days later, he rode the fifty miles to Sutter's Fort, where, after a few more tests, Sutter swore the mill boss and his other workers to secrecy. The landowner needed time to decide how to handle the discovery. But news this exciting couldn't be kept quiet; several of the men—even Sutter himself—mentioned the gold in letters to friends or while visiting nearby towns. Meanwhile, the lucky men who were building the mill spent their free time scraping gold flakes

Founded in 1776 as a Spanish mission and presidio (military fortress), San Francisco was a quiet port town in the years before the gold rush. As one resident later described, its sudden growth into a major city "would do credit to twenty years of American enterprise instead of two. . . ."

In 1852, a photographer captured this photo of James Marshall at the fateful Sutter's Mill. Marshall was unable to defend his claims near the mill from more determined prospectors and never earned a penny from the gold he discovered. The gold rush also caused the downfall of landowner John Sutter. All of his workers left to pan for gold, and an unstoppable flood of eager prospectors camped on his land, knocking down his fences and killing his cattle and sheep. Several times, he tried—unsuccessfully—to demand compensation from the government for his losses.

> *"Gold almost looks to me like a worthless toy—I have seen such vast quantities of it. A man, here in the mountains, who has not ten or twenty pounds of it, is looked upon as a poverty-stricken man."*
>
> **Dr. Benjamin Cory, in a letter to his brother, November 6, 1848**

from rock crevices with their pocketknives and combing streams and river beds for nuggets.

For several months, few outsiders believed the reports. But as more and more people visited the mill and nearby sites, they saw with their own eyes the pouches of glittering gold the men had collected. Word of mouth sparked a stampede of gold seekers, especially from the sleepy port town of San Francisco. By the end of May, businesses had closed and the streets emptied as everyone rushed to the Sacramento Valley to claim their fortune. Storekeepers locked their doors. Sailors abandoned ships. Newspapers stopped printing. Farmers left crops unharvested. Just as Benjamin Cory had fled his practice, almost every man in the area lost interest in his day-to-day profession, too tempted by the great riches in the valley. "I tell people that I can get more gold in the mountains than my conscience will permit me to charge my patients," the doctor explained. How could he resist?

Soon the news spread up and down the Pacific Coast. Trading ships that before deposited only a few settlers at a time, now arrived overflowing with gold seekers. "The population is rapidly increasing," Dr. Cory described. "News of the gold has extended like wildfire. Every ship from the Sandwich Islands, Oregon, and the Southern Coast is loaded with passengers—Oregon is *dead. . . .*" With these new arrivals came miners with experience in other gold fields, men from Mexico, Chile, and Peru. They showed the Californians how to sift dirt and water from a stream bed into a pan, swishing the contents until the heavier gold flakes had settled to the bottom. Armed with this simple method, men rushed to stake claims, and the price of a tin pan skyrocketed to as high as sixteen dollars—the going rate for an ounce of gold. The cost of other mining tools, such as shovels and picks, and supplies of food, clothing, tents, and blankets, climbed higher and higher each day.

In a letter to his brother, Dr. Cory admitted, "The first month I was in the mines, myself and partner dug out three thousand dollars apiece. . . ." Other miners were finding single nuggets as large as eight pounds or more—in one day, enough wealth to retire on, simply there for the taking! Each report seemed more fantastic than the last. In June 1848, Thomas Larkin, the United States naval agent in San Francisco had written an excited, but official letter to Secretary of State James Buchanan, notifying the government of the nation's newfound riches.

> *Sir: I have to report to the State Department one of the most astonishing excitements and state of affairs now existing in this country that, perhaps, has ever been brought to the notice of the Government. On the American fork of the Sacramento, and Feather River, another branch of the same, and the adjoining lands, there has been discovered, within the present year, a placer, a vast tract of land containing gold in small particles. This gold thus far has been taken on the bank of the river from the surface to eighteen inches in depth, and is supposed deeper, and to extend over the country. . . .*
>
> *P.S. This placer, or gold region, is situated on public land.*

With official reports in hand, in December 1848, President James Polk finally verified the discovery of gold in a speech to Congress. That was all the proof remaining skeptics needed. Almost a year after the finding at Sutter's Mill, the president's message sent a shiver of excitement across the nation—the rush was on!

Suddenly, lawyers, schoolteachers, blacksmiths, farmers, and bankers—most of whom had worked in neither a mine nor the wilderness—began preparing to travel west. They planned to hurry to California and return home within a year, bearing great riches. In the spirit of the day, Dr. Cory encouraged his brother to come join him in the gold fields. "There is no country on the face of the earth where a fortune can be made so easily as in California," he wrote.

Just getting to California seemed as if it would be the hardest part for most people. No matter how Americans looked at it, it was a long journey. Speed became the first consideration; if they didn't hurry, other miners might take all the gold. Cost had to be considered, too—not to mention the dangers of long-distance travel. The majority of "forty-niners," as

Highly Important
FROM THE
CALIFORNIA GOLD REGION.
OFFICIAL REPORTS TO GOVERNMENT
OF
GOLD FOUND IN LUMPS OF
16 and 25 Pounds !
GOLD TO AN IMMENSE AMOUNT OBTAINED BY
DIGGING AND WASHING !

As reliable sources confirmed the gold findings, reports in major newspapers such as the New York Tribune turned from skepticism to enthusiasm. Readers eagerly followed each new story.

San Francisco, September 25, 1849

Dear Father,

I arrived here safe & sound on Sunday, September 16, after a long & very tedious voyage. . . . I was quite astonished at the number of vessels in the harbor. It is estimated there are over 400 sails now lying here, the most of them entirely deserted. The gold excitement is very great. I am writing on a box in one of my shipmate's tents, in what is called Happy valley. We are surrounded on all sides by tents, as far as the eye can reach. There is hardly a spot of ground within 3 miles of San Francisco but what is covered with canvas.

My feelings upon first seeing the town I can hardly describe, the crowds of people moving in every direction, some that have been at the mines & returned with their pockets well lined, others just arrived & eager to glean every particle of news that is afloat, & every countenance filled with thought & anxiety for the future. . . . It is generally quite healthy here, with the exception of some cases of dysentery occasioned by change of diet & water, which is quite bad. I have been very careful in what I eat, since I came here, but have not felt very brisk since I landed. . . . There is no mistake but Gold is plenty here, but it requires some hard work to get it. . . . I have the utmost confidence that we can get rich here. There is every opportunity for an enterprising man to make money hand over hand, all I desire is that my health may be spared to me. . . .

Your affectionate son,
Ned T. Hosmer

In March 1849, brothers Charles and Edward Hosmer left their family in Avon, New York, for the gold fields of California. Edward traveled by boat around Cape Horn, while Charles went overland by wagon train. After rejoining in San Francisco, they wrote these optimistic letters to their family.

With the rainy winter months approaching, the brothers decided to postpone heading to the gold fields. Instead, they became merchants in the thriving city, enjoying quick profits until a conniving partner robbed them of more than eight thousand dollars. They managed to stay in business, but never fully recovered. In the fall of 1851, Charles returned to New York to press charges against the man who robbed them. Edward went prospecting in the Feather River area, but was unsuccessful as a miner.

San Francisco, September 27, 1849

Dear Parents,

As Ned & myself send a letter in the same envelope you will know we have met after a long & tedious months of travel, over a hard & tiresome journey. Thank God we are alive & well—Ned can tell of storms at sea, whales, sharks, &c. &c. While I can tell of Indians, Rocks, Mountains, Bear & Buffalo—so our tales of trial & suffering are of interest one to the other and many hearty laughs do we have together. Our journey across the desert here was a dreadful one, feed was scarce, our animals nearly perished. . . . After leaving the Sink of Mary's River, we crossed the desert & it was one truly, 45 miles without grass or water- here was a destruction of property, the like before I never imagined. Animals, wagons, provisions &c. &c. lie scattered to the four winds.

. . . The whole country to the valley of Sac[ramen]to River . . . is Red Clay & gravel. . . . Men get from 1 oz of gold upwards per day, many worn down with the journey, are excited at the prospects, & soon over do, bringing on diarrhea & therefore many are sick, not being acclimated. . . .

God bless & preserve you is the fervent wish of your affectionate son,

C. A. Hosmer

From California.

From the Boston Transcript, April 3.

INTERESTING LETTER FROM SAN FRANCISCO.— The following letter, of a recent date from San Francisco, was received by one of our most esteemed fellow-citizens from his brother, formerly American Consul at the Sandwich Islands, but now of San Francisco, and attached to one of the very first commercial houses at that place. It will be seen that the writer confirms all the wildest accounts we have yet had of the abundance of gold, of the high price of labor and provisions, and the extraordinary rise in land. These statements can be relied upon to the fullest extent, as the probity and sagacity of the writer are unquestionable:

SAN FRANCISCO, Jan. 20, 1849.

DEAR BROTHER—I suppose that ere this reaches you the excitement in the United States about California will run as high as it now does throughout the Pacific.

My partner arrived here on the 10th Nov. and I on 21st, and our sales already go above $500,000. The great excitement which prevails in Chili and Peru relative to this gold country is fast depopulating those countries of their European population. Every vessel that arrives brings many passengers and reports of everybody else winding up their affairs to join in the rush.

The quantity of goods that is pouring into the country is reducing the prices materially; still, everything is, compared with the original cost, very high. I paid a bill today for our table; it ran thus: Butter $1; sausages $1 per pound; pork 25 cents; eggs $2 a dozen; milk $1 per bottle; a box of fine salt $2; sperm candles $2 a pound; raisins $1 a pound; common lamp oil $2 a gallon; bottle of mustard (half a pound) $2, &c. &c.

For the little unfurnished one story building in which we stay—dining and sleeping in the same room—we pay $100 per month. Our cook receives $100 per month. My washwoman has condescended to do my washing for $6 per dozen. The carpenters employed on our warehouse threaten to leave unless we increase their wages above $8 per day. I paid a cartman this evening $72 for two days' work. You can judge by the quotations the quantity of money that a laboring man can obtain by a little work.

In regard to the gold, every day only adds to the surprise created by previous reports of the quantity to be had. Yesterday morning an Indian showed me a specimen of ore intermixed with a stone, weighing five pounds. He sold it for five hundred dollars! Today some Oregon farmers, who came down to obtain gold and remained a month at the mines, offered to sell me 150 pounds of gold, which they had collected. Mr. Brannon, who has the establishments for storing and selling goods at the mines, told me today that seven men took from the earth, within one hundred yards of his upper store, thirty-three thousand dollars' worth of gold in four days; and the gold was weighed by a man in his employment.

At the dry diggings $100 per day is paid to cooks.—The general impression is that from 10 to $20,000,000 will be taken from the mines the coming summer. It would not surprise me at all were it to be ten times that amount. The fact is, that it comes down from the mines *by the peck, pure gold !*

Newspapers in the East often published letters received by friends and relatives from people living in California. The glowing personal accounts of easily earned riches helped fuel the rush for gold.

the new gold seekers became known, chose the affordable method of covered wagons. They could follow the Oregon Trail as far west as Fort Hall and branch off on the California Trail, which ended in the Sacramento Valley. Or they could travel on the Santa Fe and Old Spanish Trails, looping through territory acquired in the Mexican War. One drawback to wagon travel was that they had to wait until the spring of '49 to leave. Not until late April would there be enough grass along the prairie to graze their oxen and mules.

Once on the trail, other difficulties arose. Outbreaks of cholera, which had ravaged eastern cities, became worse than ever before. The number of trail deaths escalated, as the infectious disease spread from one wagon train to the next. Hundreds of small wooden crosses made eerie trail markers for those who followed. In addition, the atmosphere in the California-bound companies was often fiercely competitive; the forty-niners weren't as willing to help their fellow travelers as other pioneers. One young girl, whose family was headed to Oregon, recalled seeing Califor-

> *"Hundreds of others were bound for California and many of them acted like they were afraid the gold would be gone before they could get there."*
>
> **Virginia Watson Applegate, recalling her 1849 trip from Springfield, Illinois, to Oregon, at the age of nine**

nia wagons overloaded with supplies, which the travelers hoped to sell for high profits in the mining camps. "Their teams often gave out and the wagons had to be left by the roadside—also provisions," she described. Instead of leaving the goods for passersby to possibly use, some of the gold prospectors "burned their wagons and poured turpentine on sacks of coffee and flour."

While the overland travelers hurried about, outfitting their wagons

This contemporary New York cartoon, titled "The Way They Go to California," made fun of the frenzied rush for the gold fields. One desperate miner, who missed boarding the overcrowded sailing ship, proclaims he will swim to California. Another takes off on a fictional rocket ship. And the rickety blimp carries a fake warning: "Each Passenger must provide a boy to hold his hair on."

SAN FRANCISCO via CHAGRES,
19th MAY.—The new and splendid steamship
CRESCENT CITY, 1,500 tons burden, Charles
Stoddard, Master, will leave for Chagres direct, from her
dock, at Pier 4 N. R. Saturday, 19th of May, at 4 o'clock.—
Passengers by this steamer will reach Panama in time for
the U. S. Pacific Mail Steamer of June.
  Passage in the After Saloon......................$150.
  Passage in the Forward Saloon.................. 115
  Passage in the Lower Cabin..................... 100
  Passage in the Steerage.......................... 80
Freight on specie, 1 per cent; merchandise, 70 cents per
foot. Eight cubic feet of baggage allowed each cabin passenger; six cubic feet each steerage passenger. No passenger secured unless paid for. Any person remitting one-
half of the amount of passage-money can secure a berth
for one week. For freight or passage, apply to
           J. HOWARD & SON, 73 South-st.
a18 1w*

FOR SAN FRANCISCO, CALIFORNIA,
direct, touching at Rio Janeiro and Valparaiso.—
The splendid A1 coppered and copper-fastened Liv-
erpool packet-ship SUSAN G. OWENS, Capt. J. O. Bar-
clay, 780 tons burden, and but five months old, is now ready
for sea, and will positively sail on the 21st of April. This
magnificent ship for speed, strength and accommodations
is unsurpassed by any vessel of her size in the world. She
can yet accommodate a limited number of passengers, who
may secure their berths by immediate application to
       BUFFUM & HANDY, 112 Broadway, N.Y.
a18 1t*

CALIFORNIA.—A respectable widow, aged 27, competent as teacher or seamstress, and willing to make
herself generally useful, wishes to join a family or company going to California, with whom she could make an
arrangement to render her services during the voyage, or
subsequently, for the passage for herself and child, between
two and three years of age; or to a merchant or person interested in business at the gold regions, who would be
willing to advance the passage money, a high per centage
will be given. A line addressed to S. L. Tribune Office,
will be promptly attended to.
                        a18 1t

By the spring of 1849, New York newspapers were filled with gold-rush-related advertisements—ship passage to California, life insurance for prospectors, and hopeful people, such as the "respectable widow, aged 27," trying to earn their way to the gold-rich land.

LIFE INSURANCE.
THE NAUTILUS INSURANCE COMPANY, 68 Wall-
st. makes insurance on life for any amount not exceeding $10,000. Profits divided annually. Risks continue to
be taken on lives of persons visiting
         CALIFORNIA,
In limited amounts, for the term of 3 years. Medical Ex-
aminers in attendance daily from 2 to 5 o'clock P.M.
           MORRIS FRANKLIN, President.
m24 1stf   PLINY FREEMAN, Actuary.

and bidding good-bye to family and friends, people near the East Coast looked to sailing ships to transport them to the gold. Over the Atlantic Ocean, around the tip of South America, and north along the Pacific Coast to San Francisco, the passage could take as little as four months or as long as nine. The forty-niners boarded the ships full of excitement and dreaming of twenty-pound nuggets. But spirits dampened when, for endless weeks, they suffered overcrowding, seasickness, rotten food, and foul water. They tired of their fellow passengers and the few amusements they could find—playing cards or checkers, rereading old newspapers, or singing popular songs.

The only faster route to California was costlier and more dangerous. In as little as six weeks, a forty-niner could sail to the Isthmus of Panama, cross the tropical, seventy-five-mile land bridge between the Atlantic and the Pacific, and board another ship to complete the trip to San Francisco. In Panama, travelers found themselves squeezing into long canoes, called bungos, which natives paddled and poled upriver, and riding pack mules on a steamy, jungle trail. For the women travelers, the mule ride was often the first time they had straddled a regular saddle. The Americans gaped at the wild monkeys, tropical birds, and exotic flowers, and worried about poisonous snakes. Their biggest worry, however, was disease. Swarms of mosquitoes carried malaria, and contaminated food and water gave them dysentery, not to mention the scares of deadly yellow fever and cholera. Almost every group who traveled through Panama faced sickness—or death.

By the time the seafarers made it to California, whether on the long

> *"You cannot get a man to haul your trunk across the street for less than five dollars. . . . You cannot get your handkerchief washed for less than a dollar; a dollar is the same here as twelve and a half cents in Ohio. This is fact."*
>
> **Dr. Benjamin Cory, San Francisco, November 1848**

oceangoing passage or via Panama, they were exhausted, out of shape, and ill prepared for the manual labor of mining. Still, get-rich-quick dreams fueled their energy. In San Francisco, which a year earlier had resembled a ghost town, they joined the throngs of excited newcomers. Before the discovery of gold, fewer than five hundred people lived in the small port. By early 1849, its population had increased to two thousand people, and before the year was out, it soared to more than twenty thousand

Among the thousands of California gold seekers were a number of freed and escaped slaves from the South who fled west hoping to start a new life.

Hundreds of new buildings rose, but brick and lumber were scarce and expensive. People created "buildings" from whatever materials they could slap together—packing crates, abandoned ships, or canvas. To meet the demand for temporary housing, vast tent cities rose near the town limits. Despite the ramshackle buildings and shortages of goods, one resident bragged, "Gold and money . . . is plenty as blackberries."

Exchanging their travel clothes for sturdy pants and flannel shirts, the new prospectors paid outrageous prices for gear and loaded up on advice. As soon as they gained their bearings in the chaotic town, they streamed to the hills to strike it rich. Here they met the Americans who had rushed overland, following the California Trail over the mountains to the gold-bearing region. In addition to the discovery at Sutter's Mill, miners found gold deposits along the Feather and Yuba Rivers in the northern Sierra Nevada as well as in the San Joaquin, Tuolumne, Stanislaus, Merced, and other rivers to the south.

By the mid-1850s, approximately five hundred ships lay abandoned and rotting in the San Francisco harbor. Once in port, their crews had run off to the gold fields. With building materials at a premium, the town's residents put the deserted ships to use by opening stores and hotels on board.

Competition among the determined miners was fierce. As Charles Hosmer, a San Francisco merchant from New York, described, "A man here has no friends but his money, unless a brother, or near relative. . . . " The Americans also worked alongside Mexican, Chinese, South American, Australian, and French miners—adventurous men who followed the scent of gold thousands of miles to California. Overcome with greed and ambition, many headstrong Americans lashed out at Indians and foreigners if they stood in the way of a rich claim. Hosmer called the most ruthless prospectors "men of iron hearts." In his words, "they came for gold and Indians are not to stop them—nor anything else, *short of death.*"

Whenever a rich deposit was struck, despite the finders' efforts to keep it secret, word inevitably spread. Small camps sprang up as other hopeful miners swarmed in to stake claims near the lucky discoverers. With odd names such as Mad Mule Gulch, Dead Man's Bar, Bedbug, and Fiddletown, many of the camps were abandoned within months for newer, hopefully richer claims, although permanent towns were hastily built, too. In less than a year, near Sutter's famous mill, Sacramento grew into a boisterous town of twelve thousand people and served as a supply point for miners journeying into the mountains.

True to the first reports, California did have millions of dollars of gold in its hills, but it wasn't enough to enrich all of the tens of thousands of prospectors who flooded in. The majority of miners found gold digging to be lonely, back-breaking work, similar to digging a ditch for ten hours a day. While doing this, they were living on a diet of greasy

Representative of the prejudice against Chinese miners, contemporary drawings often depicted them as slant-eyed, devilish men. The Chinese came to California for the same reasons as other forty-niners. Risking their lives on long sea voyages, they hoped to earn a fortune mining and bring wealth to their families.

Above: *Easily distinguished by their baggy cotton clothing and long braids (called queues) that hung down their backs, Chinese miners suffered much prejudice from other miners in California. In 1850 and 1852, the legislature enacted foreign miners' taxes, aimed at discouraging Chinese as well as Mexican miners. Banding together for support, Chinese men endured the hardships of being forced off claims and turned away from jobs.*

Left: *During the early gold rush years, women were a rare sight in California towns—and even rarer still in remote mining camps, where lawlessness, spoiled food, and cramped sleeping quarters were the rule of the day.*

salt pork, coffee, and spoiled bread. The easy pickings of surface gold, which made headlines early on, soon dwindled. Miners had to dig deeper and work harder to find the precious metal. John Snyder, who left Illinois to try his luck in the California gold fields, acknowledged some of the benefits of prospecting: "We have no bosses to grumble at us or discharge us, no taxes to pay, or no government agents to support. We go to work when and where we please and quit when we please." Still, he admitted, "the gold I would like to have, but the 'getting of it' is

Placerville, California, pictured here in 1855, was first known as Dry Diggings because miners had to cart their soil to running water to wash out the gold. The once-peaceful camp changed its name to Hangtown after a series of crimes—including a stabbing during a card game and the theft of fifty ounces of gold dust from a miner—resulted in quick executions of the suspected criminals. Eventually, the town's residents swapped that for the more respectable name of Placerville.

Most California mining camps were named by the whim of the men who founded them. Rough and Ready was established by a group of Mexican War veterans who had served under General Zachary Taylor—whose nickname was "Old Rough and Ready." Other sites earned their names from the amount of gold they produced: Rich Bar, on the Feather River, proved so true to its name that claims were limited to just ten square feet of the gold-rich gravel.

Oh, California!

I'll take my wash bowl in my hand,
And thither wind my way,
To wash the gold from out the sand
In California.

And when I get my pocket full
In that bright land of gold,
I'll have a rich and happy time:
Live merry till I'm old.

Oh, California
That's the land for me;
I'm going to Sacramento,
With my wash bowl on my knee!

One of the most popular songs during the gold rush years was "Oh, California." Sung to the tune of Stephen Foster's "Oh, Susanna," forty-niners made up countless new verses for the song as they traveled and worked.

attended with rather too much hard labor to detain me in the mines very long."

After some early success, Dr. Cory's luck also ran dry. "We wanted to find places where we could pick up, without much labor, two or three hundred dollars per day. But we were not fortunate enough to find such a place." Some miners struggled for years, convinced the next shovelful of dirt would bring their fortune. Many turned in their gear and returned home. Others stayed in California and found more traditional ways to earn a fortune. Supply stores, banks, gambling halls, and real estate sales proved extremely lucrative for more than a few hardnosed businessmen.

And from that fateful day in January 1848, at the quiet mill on the American River, the United States would never be the same. Just two years after the discovery of gold, California became the thirty-first state in the Union. By the mid-1850s, its population exceeded a quarter of a million people, causing Americans to widen their view of the country from the concentrated population of the eastern seaboard to the West Coast and the wide open spaces between. Its mineral riches caused the world to take note of the rising power of the United States.

California's sudden growth topped off an astounding fifty years in American history. Since Lewis and Clark had returned from their momentous journey, fur trappers and traders had traversed the peaks and valleys of the majestic Rocky Mountain Range. Oregon Territory had been settled and claimed for the United States. Texas had won its independence from Mexico and been annexed as the twenty-eighth state. And as a result of the Mexican War, the United States had acquired vast new lands in California and the Southwest. Now the focus turned from expansion and

July 6, 1851, East Fork, of the North Fork, Feather River

Dear Parents, Brothers & Sisters,

For the first time in four months I have just received a letter from home. I had almost despaired of ever getting one again but as I am someways from post coaches & mail rout[e]s it is not much to be wondered at. . . .

Gustavus, & Mr. Kelly, a friend of mine from Cincinnati, and myself started from San Francisco for the purpose of going to the Feather River mines & trying our luck this summer. . . . [With a] Gun on my shoulder, drinking cup in my belt, we started for Rich Bar where I am now mining. The first night we camped on the banks of the main Feather River, ate our Slap Jacks & Pork, staked out our mules & turned in, slept soundly on the fresh Grass & awoke at the dawn of day, cooked our breakfast, repacked our Mules & forward march. . . . We lost our trail once in the mountains & fortunately came across some Indians who set us right by making marks in the sand with a stick to show us the direction the different trails took. . . . We had about sixty miles to travel, snow all the day from 6 to 20 feet deep, only a narrow mule path, where a misstep would take us & our animals nearly out of sight. . . . We finally got through safely, with a snowball for a pillow at night & the mountain wolves howling around us as we slept . . . I can assure you it was anything but pleasant . . . [but] for all the fatigue, there was a sort of excitement about it that just suited me. . . .

May peace and happiness ever be with you all is the sincere wish of your absent

Ned

Edward Hosmer and his companions worked several different claims, all of which turned out to be "nearly perfect failures." In early September, Edward packed up and returned to Sacramento. Still optimistic, he wrote home: "I am young & California holds out greater inducements to a young man who has any spirit at all, than any other country in the world." Eventually, he too returned to New York.

discovery to the building of a powerful nation. To many, the coming years would bring new hopes and possibilities; for others, there would be bitter conflicts over land and the brutal effects of a wild code of frontier justice. But beyond the Mississippi lay a newly defined American West—a land whose diverse peoples and varied landscapes would play a vital and exciting role in the nation's history. ✪

Glossary

adobe   sun-dried clay, often formed into bricks for use in buildings

annexation   the incorporation of a territory into an existing state or country

annuity   a once-yearly payment of money or goods

anthropology   the scientific study of the origin, culture, and development of human beings

botany   the scientific study of plants

brigade   a group of persons with a common purpose

cede   to transfer ownership

chief factor   a head agent or top company official

cholera   an infectious, often fatal disease, characterized by vomiting, cramps, and watery diarrhea

claim   a section of public land staked out by a miner or homesteader

confluence   the place where two rivers or streams run together

conquistador   a Spanish soldier involved in the conquering of the Indian civilizations of Mexico, Central America, or Peru during the sixteenth century

Continental Divide   the high ground in the Rocky Mountains from each side of which the continent's rivers flow in opposite directions

corps   a specialized branch of the armed forces; also, a body of persons acting with a common purpose. The official title of Lewis and Clark's expedition was the Corps of Discovery.

diphtheria   a serious bacterial disease, characterized by high fever, weakness, and difficulty breathing

dominion   sovereignty, or control

dysentery   a painful, sometimes fatal disorder of the intestines, characterized by severe diarrhea

emigrant   a person who leaves one country or region to settle in another. Before Oregon and California became part of the United States, overland pioneers were called emigrants because they passed outside U.S. territory after crossing the Rocky Mountains.

garrison   a military post; to occupy as a military post

gilded   covered with a thin layer of gold

heathen   a person who follows a religion other than Christianity, Judaism, or Islam; a derogatory term, which implies that someone is uncivilized

keelboat   a riverboat used for carrying freight; similar to a barge

Manifest Destiny   the United States' belief in its God-given right to expand across the continent

missionary   a person who is sent to do religious work in a foreign land

Mormons   members of the Church of Jesus Christ of Latter-day Saints; also referred to as Saints

peso   a Mexican dollar

pilot bread   hardtack; a hard bread made with flour and water

pirogue   a large, wide, dugout canoe, constructed by carving out a solid log

polygamy   the practice of having more than one spouse at a time

portage   to carry boats and supplies overland from one water route to another

presidio   a fortress or garrison

prospector   a person who searches for deposits of metals, such as gold or silver

province   a territory governed as a unit of a country

pueblo   a village of multi-storied apartment dwellings built of adobe or stone by Native American tribes of the Southwest, including the Zuni, Taos, and Hopi Indians

rheumatism   a disease that causes pain in the muscles, joints, and tendons

smallpox   a highly infectious, often fatal disease, marked by high fever and blistering spots on the skin

squatter   a person who, without legal claim, settles on unclaimed or public land in an attempt to obtain title to it

stockade   an enclosure made of strong posts driven upright into the ground

textiles   cloth or other fabric

treaty   a formal agreement between two or more nations

tributary   a stream that flows into a larger stream or other body of water

yellow fever   an infectious tropical disease transmitted by mosquitoes, characterized by jaundice, high fever, and dark-colored vomit

Zion   a promised land or holy city

Further Reading

Bakeless, John, ed. *The Journals of Lewis and Clark*. New York: Penguin Books, 1964.

Ball, John. *Autobiography of John Ball*. Grand Rapids, Mich.: The Dean-Hicks Company, 1925.

Blumberg, Rhoda. *The Incredible Journey of Lewis and Clark*. New York: Lothrop, Lee & Shepard Books, 1987.

Bonvillain, Nancy. *Black Hawk: Sac Rebel*. New York: Chelsea House, 1994.

Brown, Joseph E. *The Mormon Trek West*. New York: Doubleday & Company, 1980.

Carter, Alden R. *The Mexican War*. New York: Franklin Watts, 1992.

Cavan, Seamus. *Lewis and Clark and the Route to the Pacific*. New York: Chelsea House, 1991.

Clayton, William. *William Clayton's Journal*. Salt Lake City: The Deseret News, 1921.

Dale, Harrison Clifford. *The Explorations of William H. Ashley and Jedediah Smith, 1822 1829*. Lincoln, Nebr.. University of Nebraska Press, 1991

Daniels, George D., ed. *The Spanish West*. (The Old West Series). New York: Time-Life Books, 1976.

Faber, Harold. *From Sea to Sea: The Growth of the United States*. New York: Charles Scribner's Sons, 1992.

Fontana, Bernard L. *Entrada: The Legacy of Spain and Mexico in the United States*. Tucson: Southwest Parks and Monuments Association, 1994.

Fort Vancouver. Handbook 113, Division of Publications, National Park Service, U.S. Dept. of the Interior, Washington, D.C., 1981.

Goetzmann, William H. *Exploration and Empire. The Explorer and the Scientist in the Winning of the American West*. New York: W. W. Norton & Company, 1966.

Holmes, Kenneth L., ed. *Covered Wagon Women: Diaries & Letters from the Western Trails 1840–1890*. Volume 1: 1840–1849. Glendale, Calif.: The Arthur H. Clark Company, 1983.

Horn, Huston, and the editors of Time-Life Books. *The Pioneers*. (The Old West Series). New York: Time-Life Books, 1974.

Jackson, Donald, ed. *Black Hawk: An Autobiography*. Urbana, Ill.: University of Illinois Press, 1955.

Jeffrey, Julie Roy. *Converting the West: A Biography of Narcissa Whitman*. Norman, Okla.: University of Oklahoma Press, 1991.

Johnson, William Weber, and the editors of Time-Life Books. *The Forty-niners*. (The Old West Series). New York: Time-Life Books, 1974.

Johnston, Abraham Robinson, Marcellus Ball Edwards, and Philip Gooch Ferguson. *Marching with the Army of the West 1846–1848*. Ed. Ralph P. Bieber. Glendale, Calif.: The Arthur H. Clark Company, 1936.

Milner, Clyde A. II, Carol A. O'Connor, and Martha A. Sandweiss, eds. *The Oxford History of the American West*. New York: Oxford University Press, 1994.

Myres, Sandra L., ed. *Ho for California! Women's Overland Diaries from the Huntington Library*. San Marino, Calif.: Henry E. Huntington Library and Art Gallery, 1980.

Nardo, Don. *The Mexican-American War*. San Diego: Lucent Books, 1991.

Nevin, David, and the editors of Time-Life Books. *The Texans*. (The Old West Series). New York: Time-Life Books, 1975.

Russell, Osborne. *Journal of a Trapper*. Portland, Ore.: Oregon Historical Society, the Champoeg Press, Reed College, 1955.

Schwantes, Carlos A. *The Pacific Northwest: An Interpretive History*. Lincoln, Nebr.: University of Nebraska Press, 1989.

Smith, Capt. E. Kirby. *To Mexico with Scott: Letters of Captain E. Kirby Smith to His Wife*. Ed. Emma Jerome Blackwood. Cambridge: Harvard University Press, 1917.

Stegner, Wallace. *The Gathering of Zion: The Story of the Mormon Trail*. New York: McGraw-Hill, 1964.

Takaki, Ronald. *A Different Mirror: A History of Multicultural America*. Boston: Little, Brown & Company, 1993.

Thwaites, Reuben Gold, ed. *Original Journals of the Lewis and Clark Expedition, 1804–1806* (7 volumes). New York: Dodd, Mead & Company, 1905.

Weber, David J. *The Spanish Frontier in North America*. New Haven, Conn.: Yale University Press, 1992.

White, Richard. *"It's Your Misfortune and None of My Own": A New History of the American West*. Norman, Okla.: University of Oklahoma Press, 1991.

Whitman, Narcissa. *The Letters of Narcissa Whitman*. Fairfield, Wash.: Ye Galleon Press, 1986.

Index

Page numbers in *italics* refer to photographs and illustrations.

Picture Credits

The photographs and illustrations in this book are from the following sources. The images are public domain or are used with the source's permission.

The source's photo or illustration identification number is listed after each page number for the Library of Congress and Oregon Historical Society listings.

Alfred A. Hart Collection, Stanford University Archives, Stanford, Calif. • page 87

Colorado Historical Society, Denver, Colo. • page 35 (both)

Denver Public Library, Western History Department, Denver, Colo. • pages 36–37, 38, 82–83

Harper's Monthly • pages 93 (bottom), 94, 95 (April, 1853)

Harper's Weekly • pages 68, 70 (May 1, 1858); 113, 123 (October 3, 1857)

Jefferson National Expansion Memorial, St. Louis, Mo. • pages 7 (top right), 9, 121, 124 (both)

Jefferson National Expansion Memorial/Kansas Historical Society, St. Louis, Mo. • page 34 (bottom)

Jefferson National Expansion Memorial/National Archives, St. Louis, Mo. • page 84

Jefferson National Expansion Memorial/National Park Service, St. Louis, Mo. • page 20

Jefferson National Expansion Memorial/Smithsonian, St. Louis, Mo. • page 122

Jefferson National Expansion Memorial/Utah State Historical Society, St. Louis, Mo. • page 92

LDS Church Historical Department, Archives, Salt Lake City, Utah • pages 91, 93 (top left), 98

Library of Congress, Washington, D.C. • pages ii, #LC-USZC4-668; 5 (top right), #LC-USZ62-2034; 6 (top left), #LC-USZ62-86; 8, #LC-USZ62-13003; 31, #LC-USZ62-2034; 60, #LC-USZ62-86; 62, #LC-USZ62-8181; 64–65, #LC-USZ62-32586; 67, #LC-USZ62-13007; 69, #LC-USZ62-43902; 96 (bottom left and bottom right); 102–103, #LC-USZ62-72S; 106 (bottom), #LC-USZ62-13011; 108, #LC-USZ62-13012; 119, #LC-USZ62-104557

Missouri Gazette and Public Advertiser • page 30 (February 13, 1822)

Missouri Historical Society, St. Louis, Mo. • pages 15 (bottom), 71

Montana Historical Society, Helena, Mont. • pages 16–17

The Museum of History & Industry, Seattle, Wash. (Photos by Howard Giske) • pages 75 (bottom), 77 (bottom)

National Archives, Washington, D.C. • pages 4 (bottom), 75 (top), 96 (top)

National Park Service, Vancouver, WA • page 42

National Park Service, Vancouver, WA (Photo by Rick Edwards) • pages 26, 34 (top)

The Newberry Library, Chicago, Ill. • page 27

New York Daily Tribune • pages 7 (top left), 106 (top) (May 12, 1846); 111 (center) (March 14, 1848); 116 (January 23, 1849); 118 (April 6, 1849); 120 (all) (April 18, 1849)

The New York Public Library, New York, N.Y. • page 114 (top)

Oregon Historical Society, Portland, Ore. • pages 4 (top), #126; 5 (bottom), #20015; 6 (top right), #88642; 7 (bottom), #12752; 10 (top), #4582, and (bottom), #13082; 13, #643; 15 (top), #92501; 21, #645; 22, #646; 24, #12121; 32–33, #50; 41, #126; 45, #245; 46–47, #38777; 48, #260; 49, #21056; 50 (left), #1645, and (right), #5922; 53 (bottom), #8342; 54, #1643; 55, #627; 57 (inset), #9794, and (top), #12760; 59, #12752; 74, #88642; 76 (top), #84101, and (bottom), #92503; 77 (top), #53563; 88 (top), #47207, and (left), #3445; 89, #63686; 101, #20015; 125, #92502

Oregon State Archives, Salem, Ore. • pages 6 (bottom), 52–53, 73

Sutter's Fort State Historical Park, Sacramento, Calif. • pages 86 (all), 114 (bottom)

Texas State Library, Archives Division, Austin, Tex. • pages 5 (top left), 6 (top center), 102 (top), 104 (both), 105, 110 (both), 111 (top)

CANADA

Columbia River

Lewis & Clark Trail

Missouri River

ROCKY MOUNTAINS

Clark's return trip

Fort Vancouver

Whitman Mission

Yellowstone River

CASCADE MOUNTAINS

Snake River

Oregon Trail

Fort Hall

Soda Springs

South Pass

Devil's Rock

Independence Rock

Scotts Bluff

Chimney Rock

Courthouse R

Sacramento River

Great Salt Lake

Fort Bridger

North Platte River

Fort Laramie

South Platte Rive

Donner Pass

California Trail

Sutter's Fort

San Francisco

SIERRA NEVADA

Colorado River

Taos

PACIFIC OCEAN

Los Angeles

Santa Fe

Santa Fe Trail

San Diego

Rio Grande River

MEXIC

Expansion of the United States 1783–1848

RED RIVER BASIN
1818

OREGON
COUNTRY
1846

LOUISIANA
PURCHASE
1803

MEXICAN
CESSION
1848

THE UNITED STATES
IN 1783

GADSDEN
PURCHASE
1853

TEXAS
ANNEXATION
1845

FLORIDA
1819